A2 Key (for Schools) test content in *Own It!* Level 2 has been checked by Cambridge Assessment English for accuracy and level.

WORKBOOK
WITH EBOOK
Annie Cornford

CAMBRIDGE
UNIVERSITY PRESS

Shaftesbury Road, Cambridge CB2 8EA, United Kingdom

One Liberty Plaza, 20th Floor, New York, NY 10006, USA

477 Williamstown Road, Port Melbourne, VIC 3207, Australia

314–321, 3rd Floor, Plot 3, Splendor Forum, Jasola District Centre, New Delhi – 110025, India

103 Penang Road, #05-06/07, Visioncrest Commercial, Singapore 238467

José Abascal, 56 – 1°, 28003 Madrid, Spain

Cambridge University Press & Assessment is a department of the University of Cambridge.

We share the University's mission to contribute to society through the pursuit of education, learning and research at the highest international levels of excellence.

www.cambridge.org
Information on this title: www.cambridge.org/9781009043526

© Cambridge University Press & Assessment 2020

First published 2020

20 19

Printed in Dubai by Oriental Press

A catalogue record for this publication is available from the British Library

ISBN 978-1-009-04352-6 Own it! Workbook with eBook Level 2
ISBN 978-84-9036-098-9 Collaborate Workbook Level 2

Additional resources for this publication at www.cambridge.org.ownit/resources

CONTENTS

WELCOME!

VOCABULARY AND READING
Free time and hobbies

1 ⭐ Match six of the phrases in the box with the photos.

> **1** chat online   2 download songs and listen to music
> **3** go shopping   **4** go for a bike ride   **5** hang out with
> friends   **6** make cakes   **7** make videos   **8** play an
> instrument   **9** read books   **10** read magazines
> **11** take photos   **12** write a blog

a b c
d e f

Sport

2 ⭐ Put the letters in the correct order to make sports words. The first letter is given.

1 b e a t l n n e t s i   table tennis
2 b r g y u   r_____
3 c t s a h i e l t   a_____
4 i s a g i l n   s_____
5 c e h o k y   h_____
6 n m a y s g t s c i   g_____
7 b y v l e l a l o l   v_____
8 s a a b b l l t e k   b_____
9 w s i g m i m n   s_____
10 s w n f i u r n g d i   w_____

A blog post

3 ⭐ Read Pablo's blog post. What is his best friend's favourite activity? _____

Home   News   **Blog**   Lifestyle   🔍

My friends and their hobbies
Hi there, Pablo here! Today my blog is about two of my friends and their hobbies.

Carla lives in an apartment in our building. We go to the same school, but we aren't in the same class. Carla loves riding her bike, so she usually cycles to school. I don't cycle when the weather's bad, but I like cycling with her in the summer. Carla also plays hockey and does gymnastics – she's very sporty!

Nico is my best friend – he's Italian. He speaks Italian at home with his family, but he doesn't speak Italian with me. He plays volleyball in our school team on Wednesday afternoons and Saturday mornings. On Sundays, we often do his favourite free-time activity: making pizzas! His dad's a chef in a pizzeria, so Nico knows a lot about pizzas – and I like eating pizzas a lot!

4 ⭐⭐ Read the blog again. Circle the correct options.
1 Carla and Pablo *go* / *don't go* to the same school.
2 Pablo *cycles* / *doesn't cycle* to school every day.
3 Carla's very *good* / *bad* at sport.
4 Pablo's best friend *speaks* / *doesn't speak* Italian.
5 Pablo likes *making* / *eating* pizzas.

Explore it!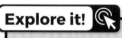

Guess the correct answer.
Marathon runners often lose height when they run a race. On average, a marathon runner is *1 cm / 5 cm / 10 cm* shorter at the end of a race.

Find another interesting fact about running. Then send a question in an email to a classmate or ask them it in the next class.

LANGUAGE IN ACTION AND VOCABULARY

Present simple

1 ☆ Complete the sentences with the present simple form of the verbs in the box.

> go   make   not see   ~~play~~   write

1 Max ____plays____ computer games every day.
2 Lena's friend _____ to a different school.
3 We _____ our friends on Sunday evenings.
4 I _____ my blog two or three times a week.
5 Martha _____ videos of her pets.

2 ☆☆ Write questions about Pablo's blog and answer them. Then check on page 4.

1 when / Pablo / cycle with Carla ?

When does Pablo cycle with Carla?
Pablo cycles with Carla in the summer.

2 what sports / Carla / do ?

_____
_____

3 where / Nico's father / work ?

_____
_____

4 what / Nico / know a lot about ?

_____
_____

Adverbs of frequency

3 ☆☆ Put the words in the correct order to make sentences.

1 computer / often / I / magazines / read

I often read computer magazines.

2 never / hockey / her / Iris / late / class / is / for

_____

3 takes / photos / great / always / Paul

_____

4 sometimes / next / Molly / to / friend / sits / her

_____

5 music / you / listen / Do / to / usually / loud / ?

_____

Personal possessions

4 ☆☆ Find the ten personal possessions in the photos in the wordsearch. Tick (✓) the photos when you find the words.

T	N	O	H	M	C	H	S	A	L	J	N
A	Z	Q	S	O	I	B	C	D	S	G	H
B	U	R	R	N	O	A	L	H	S	S	J
L	Y	D	K	E	Y	S	H	E	F	C	H
E	F	M	W	Y	R	P	S	A	O	H	G
T	V	L	S	I	E	T	D	D	P	A	C
F	K	S	C	P	A	S	S	P	O	R	T
K	V	W	J	H	D	S	U	H	R	G	O
L	A	P	T	O	P	D	B	O	T	E	S
O	B	U	P	N	L	P	D	N	A	R	A
U	(C	A	M	E	R	A)	C	E	B	R	L
T	E	Y	N	J	A	N	W	S	L	E	G
D	S	K	L	H	Q	L	D	A	E	D	F
B	U	S	P	A	S	S	P	N	M	O	V

LISTENING AND LANGUAGE IN ACTION

A conversation

🎧 **1** S.01 ⭐ **Listen and ⊙circle the correct option.**

Hannah meets Mrs Hayes at the *shops / sports club / bus stop*.

🎧 **2** S.01 ⭐⭐ **Listen again. Tick (✓) the activities that Hannah and Joe do.**

	Gymnastics class	Athletics club	Photography club	Play video games
Hannah	✓			
Joe	✗			

🎧 **3** S.01 ⭐⭐ **Listen again. Are the sentences *T* (true) or *F* (false)?**

1 Mrs Hayes likes doing sport at the weekend. _____F_____

2 Joe goes to athletics club on Saturday evenings. _____

3 The gymnastics class is one and a half hours. _____

4 The school's photography club is once a week. _____

5 Joe likes writing video games. _____

6 Hannah does her homework at the weekend. _____

love, like, don't mind, hate + -ing

4 ⭐⭐ **Complete the sentences with the correct form of the verbs in the box.**

> ~~be~~   help   play   speak   use   write

1 Susie hates ____being____ late for class, so she always arrives early.

2 Harry doesn't mind _____ football, but it's not his favourite sport.

3 I love _____ English, so I often phone my English cousins.

4 Do you like _____ headphones when you listen to music?

5 Bella loves _____ her blog. It's really good and we all read it.

6 Good friends don't mind _____ you when you've got a problem.

have got

5 ⭐⭐ **Complete the questions and short answers with the correct form of *have got*.**

1 A ____Have____ you ____got____ your own computer?

   B Yes, ____I have____.

2 A _____ Jack _____ his own keys?

   B Yes, _____.

3 A _____ Enzo and Lou _____ a French mother?

   B No, _____.

4 A _____ I _____ the right phone number for you?

   B No, _____.

5 A _____ we _____ any maths homework today?

   B Yes, _____.

6 A _____ your mum _____ a new laptop?

   B Yes, _____.

6 ⭐⭐ **⊙Circle the correct options to complete the email.**

● ● ●

Hi Leo,

I [1]*'ve got* / *'s got* some exciting news. We [2]*'ve got / haven't got* new neighbours and there's a girl called Jessica – she's my new friend. [3]*Have we got / We have got* a lot in common? Yes, we [4]*haven't / have*! She's my age and she [5]*'s got / 've got* long dark hair, just like me. She loves [6]*listen / listening* to music and singing, and she [7]*'s got / hasn't got* her own band – so cool! She [8]*haven't got / hasn't got* any sisters or brothers, but I don't mind [9]*to share / sharing* my annoying little brothers with her! Jessica and I [10]*love / hate* hanging out together already!

See you soon!
Anita

WRITING
A personal profile

1 ⭐ **Read Bruna's profile of her brothers. When are they all free to hang out together?**

HOME   **ABOUT ME**   ARCHIVE   FOLLOW

1 Hi! My name's Bruna and this profile is about my two brothers. We're from São Paulo, in Brazil. My brothers are called Victor and Lucas. Victor's 9 years old and Lucas is 12. I'm 14.

2 Lucas is mad about football, like lots of people in Brazil! He trains on Mondays, Wednesdays, Fridays and Saturdays! He never minds getting home late because he just loves playing. Victor's favourite free-time activity is swimming. He's got a great coach and he gets up early for lessons with her in the pool at the sports centre.

3 Lucas and Victor also like playing table tennis, and we all love doing that together. We've got a table tennis table in our garage and we often have a game on Sundays, when we're all free. I sometimes find Lucas annoying, but he's usually good fun, and Victor is OK. Have you got brothers and sisters? What are they like?

2 ⭐⭐ **Read the profile again. Are the sentences *T* (true) or *F* (false)?**

1 Lucas and Victor have got one sister. T

2 Lucas does part of his football training at the weekend. ___

3 Lucas never gets home late from training. ___

4 Victor prefers table tennis to swimming. ___

5 Bruna doesn't play table tennis with her brothers. ___

3 ⭐⭐ **Read the profile again. <u>Underline</u> one example of …**

1 's for possession   3 's for *is*

2 's for *has*   4 commas in a list

4 ⭐⭐ **Rewrite the text with contractions, apostrophes and commas in your notebook.**

My friend Mason has got a big family. He has got two brothers two sisters and 35 cousins. They all live in the same street! In Masons house there are a lot of pets. They have got two dogs three cats four rabbits and a parrot! They have got a big house and a big garden, so there is lots of space!

Write a profile of a friend or a family member.

PLAN
5 ⭐⭐ **Make notes for each paragraph.**

1 His/Her family and friends

2 His/Her favourite free-time activity
   • what it is and where he/she does it
   • how often he/she does it

3 Other free-time activities
   • what he/she likes doing on his/her own or with friends
   • when and where he/she does the activities

WRITE
6 ⭐⭐⭐ **Write your profile. Remember to include three paragraphs, the information in Exercise 5, the present simple, adverbs of frequency, *love*, etc. + *-ing* and *have got*.**

CHECK
7 **Do you …**
   • describe the family and friends of the person in your profile?
   • explain his/her favourite free-time activity?
   • say what else he/she likes doing, and when?

1 WHAT ARE YOU WATCHING?

VOCABULARY
TV shows

1 ⭐ **Complete the words with the missing vowels.**

1 o n-d e m a n d s e r i e s
2 sp _ rts sh _ w
3 d _ c _ m _ nt _ ry
4 dr _ m _
5 g _ m _ sh _ w
6 ch _ t sh _ w

7 s _ _ p _ p _ r _
8 th _ n _ ws
9 c _ m _ dy
10 c _ _ k _ ry sh _ w
11 c _ rt _ _ n
12 r _ _ l _ ty sh _ w

2 ⭐ ⟨Circle⟩ **the correct options.**

1 What is the first prize on the TV *drama* / ⟨*game show*⟩ this week?
2 Dan loves food, so he watches all the *sports* / *cookery* shows.
3 Adele is talking to some other guests on tonight's *soap opera* / *chat show*.
4 We always laugh a lot at the new *drama* / *comedy* on Channel 4 because it's really funny.
5 Sam watches *the news* / *an on-demand series* to learn about world events.
6 Now they use computers to make *documentaries* / *cartoons*. They don't draw them by hand.

3 ⭐ **Match the definitions with TV shows in Exercise 1.**

1 a programme about a subject, like history or nature
   documentary
2 information about real world events _____
3 information about tennis, football, basketball, etc.
   _____
4 an animated story, usually for younger people
   _____
5 a programme in which you answer questions and win a prize
   _____
6 a programme about real people in their ordinary lives
   _____

4 ⭐⭐ **Complete the text about Elena's family with the words in the box.**

chat shows   comedies   cookery shows
~~dramas~~   on-demand series   soap operas

My parents enjoy watching TV
¹ _dramas_ , especially when they are true stories from history. They both like
² _____ with famous chefs, too. My dad also enjoys
³ _____ on late-night TV. They make him laugh, but I don't think his favourite shows are funny at all! My mum watches ⁴ _____ with interesting celebrities talking about their latest films, and I sometimes watch them with her. My grandma enjoys her favourite ⁵ _____ because she knows all the characters and is interested in their lives. I usually prefer
⁶ _____ to regular TV programmes because I can watch them when I want to. I love that!

Explore it!

Guess the correct answer.
Blue Peter, the oldest children's TV show in the world, is about *40 / 60 / 80* years old.

Find an interesting fact about a TV show in your country. Then send a question in an email to a classmate or ask them it in the next class.

READING

Tweets

1 ⭐ Read the tweets. Which tweeter isn't very happy?

_____

2 ⭐⭐ Read the tweets again and check the meaning of these words in a dictionary. Then complete the sentences.

> billion   ~~competitor~~   fact   live   support

1 Gina's not a _competitor_, she's watching the event on TV today.

2 There's an interesting _____ about on-demand series in this article.

3 More than 2 _____ people watch the World Cup Final on TV. That's more than 2,000 million people!

4 The game's on _____ – all the action is happening now.

5 Which team on tonight's game show do you _____?

3 ⭐⭐ Read the tweets again and answer the questions.

1 At what time can people watch the UEFA Champions League Final live?

at eight o'clock

2 What doesn't Mehmet want to watch?

_____

3 Where is Amy today?

_____

4 What sport does Amy like playing?

_____

5 What can people watch on Channel 1 at the moment?

_____

6 Where is Antonio today?

_____

4 ⭐⭐⭐ Answer the questions with your own ideas.

1 Do you prefer doing sport or watching it on TV? Why?

_____

2 Do you ever watch sports live? Which ones?

_____

 Channel1 Sport @channel1sport
It's the day of the UEFA Champions League Final, and you can see it live on our sports show from eight o'clock tonight or later on demand from 11! More than 4 billion people watch football on TV. Are you one of them? Tweet us and tell us: are you watching or doing sport right now?

 Mehmet Ersoy @MErsoy
I want to watch basketball on TV today, but my sister's here with her friend. They're sitting in the living room and watching a really bad comedy show! So I'm watching my series in the kitchen on a tiny tablet!

 Amy Mount @aMount
I'm sitting in my friend's house and we're waiting for the big final to begin on Channel 1. We love watching sport on TV. We often play football too, but today we're eating snacks and supporting our team.

 Channel1 Sport @channel1sport
Right now on Channel 1, we're looking at the Olympics with a documentary about its history. Here's an interesting fact: around 3.5 billion people watched the Rio Olympics! But what do you think – do more people watch the Olympics or the World Cup Final? Which other sports are good to watch on TV?

 Antonio González @toni2020
I think cycling's a great sport to watch on TV, but today I'm standing at the side of the road watching the competitors in my country's famous three-week event: the _Vuelta a España_! They're doing a very long part of the race today: over 200 km in one day!

LANGUAGE IN ACTION
Present continuous

1 ⭐ Circle the correct options.

1 In my school, we *learning* / *'re learning* how to edit videos.

2 Leni *is making* / *is makeing* clothes for the school production.

3 Helena and Jez *are watch* / *are watching* their favourite programme.

4 Who *is sitting* / *is siting* next to you in class today?

5 My brother *isn't eating* / *not eating* much at the moment.

6 *Are you waiting* / *You waiting* for the news to begin?

2 ⭐ Complete the sentences with the present continuous form of the verbs in brackets.

1 She _'s chatting_ (chat) to her friends online.

2 He _____ (prepare) his history presentation.

3 We _____ (wait) for the school bus.

4 He _____ (make) a video about skateboarders.

5 They _____ (not cry); they _____ (laugh).

6 I _____ (not watch) anything; I _____ (work)!

3 ⭐⭐ Put the words in the correct order to make questions. Then match them with the answers in Exercise 2.

a those / crying / are / Why / boys / ?

Why are those boys crying? ⑤

b on the computer / Anita / doing / What / is / ?

_____ ☐

c you / there / all / Why / standing / are / ?

_____ ☐

d park / doing / the / Amir / What / is / in / ?

_____ ☐

e Why / late / working / is / tonight / Paul / ?

_____ ☐

f you / What / watching / are / on TV / ?

_____ ☐

4 ⭐⭐ Write questions and short answers with the present continuous.

1 you / cycle / to school? (✔)

Are you cycling to school? ____ Yes, I am. ____

2 we / listen / to the instructor? (✗)

_____

3 she / wait / for the next episode? (✔)

_____

4 they / enjoy / the programme? (✗)

_____

5 you / send / a message to a friend? (✗)

_____

6 I / help / you? (✔)

_____

5 ⭐⭐ Complete the email with the correct present continuous form of the verbs in the box.

| learn look forward to ~~not use~~ prepare |
| take use work write |

● ● ●

Hi Uncle Dom,

Mum tells me you've got a new camera and that you want to give me your old one because you ¹ _aren't using_ it. Great! I hear it's better than the one I ² _____ at the moment, so I ³ _____ this email to say thank you! ⁴ _____ you _____ lots of great photos now with your new camera?

I ⁵ _____ a presentation for my media studies class with a classmate this week. We ⁶ _____ a lot about taking photos in black and white – it's interesting! We ⁷ _____ on a series of winter photos. So I ⁸ _____ the new camera very much!

Thanks again and see you soon,

Jo

VOCABULARY AND LISTENING
Making movies

1 ⭐ **Complete the crossword. Use the clues.**

Down

1 Marius is writing the … for his documentary project.
2 Where are they building the … for the new soap opera?
4 The best … in *The Hunger Games* is Josh Hutcherson.
6 A … artist called Lucy is making that young woman look older.
7 The … is just sitting in her chair and telling us what to do.
9 I can take great photos with my new digital … .

Across

3 Please move those … . They're shining in my eyes.
5 I'm wearing a gorilla … and I'm getting very hot!
8 A sound … knows when the actors are too quiet or too loud.
10 I'm hoping to be a camera … when I leave school.

2 ⭐ **Match 1–5 with a–e.**

1 She's a top make-up artist ☐b
2 You can take hundreds of photos ☐
3 The sound engineer ☐
4 Steven Spielberg ☐
5 The studio goes dark ☐

a is a famous film director.
b and she can change actors' appearances.
c when the lights go out.
d is wearing big headphones.
e with a digital camera.

A guided tour

🎧 3 ⭐⭐ **Listen to a girl on a tour of a soap opera set and answer the questions.**
1.01

1 In which city do they film the soap opera? _____
2 How many families are in the soap opera? _____
3 What is the street in the soap opera called? _____

🎧 4 ⭐⭐ **Listen again and (circle) the correct answers.**
1.01

1 What is the name of the soap opera?
   a *Best Mates*   b *Teenlife*   c *Time of Our Lives*
2 One of the main actors is called … .
   a Jamie Johnson   b Tom Bridges   c Lauren Thomas
3 The soap opera is about … .
   a teenagers' lives   b a postman   c a school in Sydney
4 There are … houses in Clifton Street.
   a 15   b 20   c 100
5 There are … actors in the soap opera.
   a 10   b 50   c 60

5 ⭐⭐⭐ **Answer the questions.**
1 Which series do you like?
_____

2 What are the most popular soap operas in your country?
_____

LANGUAGE IN ACTION
Present simple and present continuous

1 ⭐ Complete the table with the time expressions in the box.

> ~~always~~   at the moment   every day
> every week   never   right now
> this afternoon   today

Present simple	Present continuous
always	

2 ⭐ Complete the sentences with the present simple or present continuous form of the verbs in brackets.

1 She __'s waiting__ (wait) for her favourite TV show to start.
2 Actors _____ (love) taking selfies with their fans.
3 It usually _____ (take) days to learn the words of a script.
4 We _____ (watch) the news together at the moment.
5 I _____ (not come) here very often.
6 They _____ (make) a new episode every week.

3 ⭐⭐ Put the words in the correct order to make sentences.

1 download / Internet / Do / always / from / you / the / films / ?

Do you always download films from the Internet?

2 drama / good / I'm / the / a / moment / TV / watching / at

_____

3 outside / eat / sometimes / summer / We / lunch / our / the / in

_____

4 talks / actors / to / sound engineer / the / The / never

_____

5 you / listening / teacher / your / now / right / Are / to / ?

_____

6 now / taking / Sydney / guided tour / a / My / is / sister / of

_____

Adverbs of manner

4 ⭐⭐ <u>Underline</u> and correct one mistake in each sentence.

1 My mother isn't a <u>slowly</u> driver. ____slow____
2 Their little brothers are playing happyly.

_____

3 Our parents teach us to say 'thank you' nice.

_____

4 Be carefully! That camera is very expensive!

_____

5 You're doing your homework very good at the moment. _____
6 She's playing the guitar beautiful now.

_____

5 ⭐⭐ Choose the correct adjectives. Then complete the sentences with the adverb forms.

1 My brother writes very ___well___ (good / bad). I enjoy reading his stories.
2 Leila speaks very _____ (loud / quiet). I can't hear what she's saying sometimes.
3 That film starts _____ (slow / fast). The beginning is really boring.
4 Kitty is singing really _____ (loud / quiet). You can hear her in the street!
5 You work _____ (easy / hard). That's why you do well in your tests.
6 This book ends _____ (good / bad). I don't like the ending at all.

WRITING
A description of a celebrity

1 ⭐ Read the description. Why can you watch Mason Millerson videos with your parents?

_____

My favourite comedian
By Kerem Uzun

1 Mason Millerson is my favourite comedian. He's an Australian comedian, internet personality, singer, writer and actor. His comedy videos have got over 2 billion views and he has over 15 million subscribers.

2 In each video, Mason is really funny and very original. You can watch his videos on the Internet. In them, he just speaks to the camera in a very natural way and you're laughing all the time. Sometimes I laugh so much that I cry! He talks about ordinary, everyday things like eating dinner with family or waiting for a train, but he makes them special.

3 I really like Mason Millerson because he's got a great imagination. His stories are funny, but they are never horrible or offensive, so it's OK to watch Mason's videos with your parents. I think he's great!

2 ⭐⭐ Read the description again and answer the questions.
1 Where is Mason from? _____
2 How many people watch Mason's videos online regularly? _____
3 What sometimes happens when Kerem watches Mason's videos? _____

3 ⭐ Match the start of each paragraph (a–c) with the topics (1–3).
a In each video, Mason is … ☐
b I really like Mason Millerson because … ☐
c Mason Millerson is my favourite comedian. ☐

1 an introduction to the person and his videos
2 what the person's videos are usually about
3 why I like this person

4 ⭐ Complete the sentences from the description and match them with the rules (a–c).
1 He's an Australian comedian, internet personality, singer, writer _____ actor. ☐
2 He talks about ordinary, everyday things … , _____ he makes them special. ☐
3 His stories are … never horrible _____ offensive. ☐

a We use _but_ to show different information.
b We use _or_ when there is a choice of two or more things.
c We use _and_ to add similar information.

Write a description of your favourite comedian or comedy actor.

PLAN
5 ⭐⭐ Make notes about these things.
1 Who the person is: _____
What he/she does: _____
How many followers he/she has got:
_____
2 What he/she usually does in his/her videos or films: _____
3 Why you like this person and his/her videos or films: _____

WRITE
6 ⭐⭐⭐ Write your description. Remember to include three paragraphs, the correct present tenses and adverbs, and _and_, _but_ and _or_.

CHECK
7 Do you …
• use sentences with _and_, _but_ and _or_?
• give information about what the person usually does?
• explain why you like the person?

VOCABULARY

1 **Match 1–8 with a–h.**

1 I don't like cookery shows ☐
2 We're listening to the match ☐
3 Disney is famous for ☐
4 Dad's watching a comedy, ☐
5 Ava's watching the documentary ☐
6 I love historical dramas about ☐
7 You can win a lot of money ☐
8 Do you usually watch the news ☐

a about animals in Africa.
b on some of these game shows.
c on TV or online?
d but he doesn't think it's funny.
e children's cartoons.
f on our favourite sports show.
g life in the 1500s.
h because I hate cooking.

2 **Complete the sentences with the words in the box.**

> actor   camera operator   costume   digital camera   director   lights
> make-up artist   script   set   sound engineer

1 The _____ is filming the pandas up close and getting some great shots.
2 Carlos learns the words by reading his _____ many times.
3 Does a TV news reader wear normal clothes or a _____ ?
4 The movie _____ tells everyone what to do and how to do it.
5 It can be very hot when you work under bright studio _____ .
6 The _____ for my favourite series is a street in New Zealand.
7 A _____ changes people's appearances for movies.
8 The _____ knows when the actors are speaking very quietly.
9 The _____ who plays the son is only six years old.
10 I can make great home videos with my new _____ .

LANGUAGE IN ACTION

3 **Complete the conversation with the present continuous form of the verbs in brackets.**

AYAZ What ¹_____ (you / do)?

ELIF I ²_____ (write) an email to my uncle. He ³_____ (work) on a film set at the moment.

AYAZ Wow! ⁴_____ (he / film) any famous actors?

ELIF No, he isn't. He ⁵_____ (travel) with the film crew and actors and he ⁶_____ (cook) their food. He's a chef.

AYAZ That's cool. So why ⁷_____ (you / send) him an email?

ELIF I ⁸_____ (hope) he can come to my birthday party and cook something good for me!

4 Complete the sentences with the present simple or present continuous form of the verbs in brackets.

1 I _____ (write) to my friend in Ankara right now. I _____ (email) her every month.

2 We usually _____ (watch) the news on TV, but today we _____ (listen) to it in the car.

3 Henry _____ (save) his pocket money at the moment because he _____ (need) a new bike.

4 _____ you _____ (look) for my sister? She usually _____ (sit) over there.

5 Our mum _____ (not go) to work on Fridays, but she _____ (work) today.

6 My friends _____ (swim) in the sea today, but I'm not. I _____ (prefer) swimming pools.

7 _____ you _____ (wait) for Susie? She _____ usually _____ (not arrive) late.

8 I _____ (cook) pancakes for breakfast at the moment. I often _____ (make) them at the weekend.

5 (Circle) the correct options.

1 Please be *quiet / quietly*! Your baby sister is sleeping.

2 Sandra is a very *nice / nicely* girl, in my opinion.

3 The children are watching *Frozen 2* and eating ice creams *happy / happily*.

4 I always speak *loud / loudly*, but Grandad still can't hear me.

5 When we work *quick / quickly*, we sometimes make mistakes.

6 He answered the questions *good / well* in the test.

7 Our music teacher plays the guitar *beautiful / beautifully*.

8 Catalina is wearing a very *pretty / prettily* costume in the show.

6 Complete the conversation with the missing words. (Circle) the correct options.

ANA Hi, Dan. [1]_____ your holiday?

DAN We [2]_____ a great time here. I [3]_____ with my friends and their family in their summer apartment.

ANA That's [4]_____. What do you think of it?

DAN It's [5]_____ and there's a pool.

ANA Lucky you! [6]_____ swimming every day?

DAN Well, my friends Tess and Rob [7]_____ every morning before breakfast.

ANA Great!

DAN Yeah, but actually I [8]_____ eating something first.

ANA Really?

DAN I'm always [9]_____ when I [10]_____ up!

ANA So when do you [11]_____ breakfast?

DAN Well, that's breakfast time for me – when I [12]_____ up.

1	a Enjoy you	b Are you enjoying	c You enjoy
2	a have	b has	c 're having
3	a 'm staying	b stay	c staying
4	a nice	b nicily	c nicely
5	a beautifully	b beautiful	c beautifuly
6	a Are you go	b Go you	c Do you go
7	a swims	b are swiming	c swim
8	a prefer	b 'm preferring	c 'm prefer
9	a hungrily	b hungry	c hungryly
10	a 'm waking	b wakes	c wake
11	a usually eat	b eat usually	c usual eat
12	a 'm getting	b gets	c get

VOCABULARY
The weather

1 ⭐ **Find 12 more weather words in the word snake.**

snowyfoggycoldwindyhoticycloudyrainywarmsunnywetstormydry

2 ⭐ Circle **the correct options.**

1 We've got winter coats because it is a cold / warm day.

2 Be careful, don't run! The paths are hot / icy.

3 It's not great to go skiing in rainy / snowy weather.

4 The bus driver can't see the road. It's very windy / foggy today.

5 **A** Is it raining now? **B** No, but it's wet / cloudy.

6 Trees sometimes break in very windy / warm weather.

3 ⭐⭐ **Complete the sentences with the words in the box. Then match them with photos a–f.**

foggy snowy ~~stormy~~ sunny wet windy

1 It's dangerous to go surfing in ___stormy___ weather. [f]

2 We can't have a picnic today. The grass is very _____ because of the rain. ☐

3 It's _____ and they are lost because they can't see. ☐

4 On a _____ day, they wear their hats, gloves and scarves. ☐

5 This _____ weather is perfect for going sailing. ☐

6 It's _____, so don't forget your sunglasses! ☐

4 ⭐⭐ **Complete the email with words from Exercise 1.**

● ● ●

TO: Geri
FROM: Calum

Hi Geri,

What's the weather like where you are? Here it's lovely and [1]___sunny___ and I'm sitting under a tree, with a sun hat and sunglasses on. There's no rain, so the fields are very [2]_____. I like [3]_____ weather – about 20 °C is fine, but 35 °C is very [4]_____ and not great for me! We usually get a lot of [5]_____ days in Scotland, so it's often very wet, but not this year. Actually, I can't wait for the winter, with some nice [6]_____ weekends for skiing.

Speak soon,
Calum

5 ⭐⭐ **Write the noun forms of the adjectives.**

1 rainy _____rain_____

2 cloudy _____

3 icy _____

4 sunny _____

5 windy _____

6 snowy _____

7 foggy _____

8 stormy _____

Explore it! 🖱️

Guess the correct answer.

The Sami people live in the far north of Norway, Sweden, Finland and Russia. Language experts say that the Sami have at least 8 / 18 / 180 words for snow and ice.

Find another interesting fact about the Sami people. Then send a question in an email to a classmate or ask them it in the next class.

READING
Diary extracts

1 ⭐ **Read the text and diary extracts. What did Ollie and Jack find on their journey?**

_____

Looking for treasure

In 2010, an American man hid a big box full of treasure somewhere in the Rocky Mountains. His name is Forrest Fenn and he was over 80 years old at the time. Fenn is an art expert, and he had a lot of old and very expensive objects. He filled his box with jewellery, diamonds and gold, and then buried it in a secret place in the mountains. Why did he do that? He wanted to give families a reason to enjoy time in nature. In his opinion, children spend a lot of time on computers and need to do more outdoor activities. The result? Thousands of people are looking for Forrest Fenn's treasure. Below are diary extracts from two young treasure hunters.

Ollie's diary: 10 December, 2018

We're on holiday in Yellowstone National Park and we're looking for buried treasure with our parents. They planned this trip because they wanted us to enjoy hiking and camping in the winter. Jack and I just want to find the box! Forrest Fenn wrote a 24-line poem with clues about where to find it. He shared the poem on Instagram, so we know the box is somewhere in Wyoming or Colorado – two of the BIGGEST STATES in the USA!

Jack's diary: 19 December, 2018

Time to go home, but the roads are closed and there's deep snow everywhere. We're staying in a small hostel because it's not possible to camp in this weather. It's very cold and there's no wi-fi here. And the worst thing is that we didn't find any treasure! I don't think this was a good idea after all!

2 ⭐⭐ **Read the text and diary extracts again and check the meaning of these words in a dictionary. Then complete the sentences.**

> clues bury hides ~~jewellery~~
> secret treasure

1 That ___jewellery___ shop sells beautiful earrings, necklaces and bracelets.

2 That dog is making a hole in the ground to _____ the ball!

3 She usually _____ her diary under her bed at night.

4 Grandma keeps her diamond ring in a _____ place in her house.

5 They found a ship under the sea with lots of _____ in it.

6 I always read the _____ carefully when I'm doing a crossword puzzle.

3 ⭐⭐ **Read the text again. Are the sentences *T* (true) or *F* (false)?**

1 Forrest Fenn hid expensive jewellery and gold in a box.   T

2 He hid the box because he doesn't want people to find it.   ___

3 The boys' parents didn't go with them.   ___

4 Fenn's clues are on the Internet.   ___

5 The boys can't get home because of the weather.   ___

6 Jack enjoyed hunting for treasure.   ___

4 ⭐⭐⭐ **Answer the questions with your own ideas.**

1 What outdoor activities do you do?

_____

2 Do you like the idea of this 'treasure hunt'? Why / Why not?

_____

LANGUAGE IN ACTION
Past simple

1 ⭐ **Complete the sentences with the past simple form of the verbs in brackets.**

1 The boys ___hiked___ (hike) for nine days.

2 They _____ (take) Fenn's clues with them.

3 They _____ (enjoy) listening to the poem about the buried treasure.

4 The adults and children _____ (read) the clues carefully.

5 Some people _____ (write) diaries about their journey.

6 Actually, the diary extracts _____ (be) very interesting.

2 ⭐⭐ **Complete the questions with the words in the box. Then match the questions with the answers in Exercise 1.**

did (x2)   write   hike   were   enjoy

a What ___did___ the adults and children read carefully? [4]

b How long did the boys _____ for? ▢

c _____ the diary extracts boring? ▢

d What did they _____ listening to? ▢

e What _____ they take with them? ▢

f What did some people _____? ▢

3 ⭐⭐ **Write questions and short answers in the past simple.**

1 you / have a good holiday, Tina? (✓)

Did you have a good holiday, Tina?   _Yes, I did._

2 you / swim in the sea? (✗)

_____

3 you all / go in the pool? (✓)

_____

4 your friends / like the food? (✓)

_____

5 Tomas / take lots of photos? (✓)

_____

6 Susie / want to come home? (✗)

_____

4 ⭐⭐ <u>Underline</u> **and correct one mistake in each sentence.**

1 Henry <u>seed</u> photos of the pioneers yesterday.
___saw___

2 We didn't enjoyed the bus journey. _____

3 Did you found a good tour guide last week?
_____

4 I did went out in the stormy weather. _____

5 They stopped for food and drink. _____

6 Did she be late for class yesterday? _____

5 ⭐⭐ **Complete the conversation with the correct past simple form of the verbs in the box.**

become   decide   look after   not have
return   ride   s̶e̶e̶   stay   travel   write

IVAN [1] ___Did___ you ___see___ the TV documentary about Dervla Murphy last night?

DARIA No, I didn't. Who is she?

IVAN An amazing traveller and travel writer. In 1963, she [2] _____ to cycle from her home town in Ireland all the way to India. And in those days, people [3] _____ the kinds of bikes we have now!

DARIA [4] _____ she _____ her bike all the way to India?

IVAN Yes, she did, and she [5] _____ there for a year. She [6] _____ Tibetan refugee children, and when she [7] _____ home, she [8] _____ her first book. She quickly [9] _____ a famous travel writer – there are more than 20 books by her. Dervla [10] _____ all over the world when she was younger, but she still can't drive a car!

VOCABULARY AND LISTENING

Useful objects

A radio programme

1 ⭐ Put the letters in the correct order to make words for useful objects.

1 r r r o i m   _mirror_
2 m p l a
3 l k t e b n a
4 o n o p s
5 i n f e k
6 w p l o l i
7 w b l o
8 k r o f
9 b c m o
10 l e t p a
11 s s s s o c i r
12 u p c
13 b h i r a u s h r
14 h t b t u h o s o r

2 ⭐⭐ Match the photos with six words from Exercise 1.

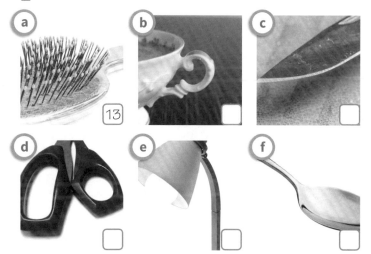

3 ⭐ Where do you usually find the objects in Exercise 1? Some words can go in more than one category.

Kitchen	Bathroom	Bedroom
knife	hairbrush	blanket

🎧 **4** ⭐ Listen to a radio programme about a volcanic
2.01 eruption. Tick (✓) the words you hear.

fork ☐   scissors ☐   comb ☐   jewellery ☐
museum ☐   schools ☐   mirror ☐   lamp ☐

🎧 **5** ⭐⭐ Listen again and complete the sentences.
2.01

1 Sam works at a __history museum__ in London.
2 The volcano destroyed two cities in
_____ hours.
3 In the _____, archaeologists found
a lot of everyday objects buried in the cities.
4 In one of the cities they found a baby's
_____ .
5 One man died when a rock hit him on the
_____ .
6 Under his body they found a purse with money
and a _____ .

6 ⭐⭐⭐ Choose from the options and complete
the sentences so they are true for you.

1 _I'd like / I wouldn't like_ to visit Pompeii and
Herculaneum because _____
_____ .
2 _I'd like / I wouldn't like_ to visit Sam's display in
London because _____
_____ .

LANGUAGE IN ACTION
there was/there were

1 ⭐ (Circle) **the correct options.**

1 (There was) / There were a team of archaeologists in Naples.

2 There was / There were some kitchen furniture in the exhibition.

3 Was there / Were there any travellers in the storm?

4 There wasn't / There weren't any information about the objects.

5 Was there / Were there a school in Herculaneum?

6 There was / There were some old books in the box.

7 There wasn't / There weren't any clothes in the ruins.

2 ⭐⭐ **Put the words in the correct order to make sentences.**

1 wasn't / rain / month / There / any / last

   There wasn't any rain last month.

2 display / any / There / the / weren't / interesting / in / things

   _____

3 people / exhibition / there / the / at / many / Were / ?

   _____

4 old / baby / with / an / woman / There / a / was

   _____

5 there / box / Was / any / the / jewellery / in / ?

   _____

6 Naples / hundreds / were / in / tourists / There / of

   _____

3 ⭐ **Match 1–6 with a–f.**

1 There were some	⌷e⌷	a	interesting display of jewellery.
2 Was there a	⌷ ⌷	b	information about Herculaneum?
3 There weren't any	⌷ ⌷	c	useful objects in the kitchen?
4 There was an	⌷ ⌷	d	women in the team.
5 Was there any	⌷ ⌷	e	Roman bowls in the museum.
6 Were there any	⌷ ⌷	f	mirror in the woman's bag?

4 ⭐⭐ **Complete the email with *some*, *any*, *a* or *an*.**

● ● ●

TO: Lily

FROM: Tom

Hi Lily!

How are you? Just a quick email to tell you about our trip to Brazil! Yesterday there was ¹ ___a___ big storm, so we had a day of culture. We walked around the city and there was ² _____ fascinating museum called the Museum of Tomorrow, so we decided to go in. It's ³ _____ science museum in Rio, but ⁴ _____ architect from Spain designed it. There were ⁵ _____ amazing exhibitions about our planet, and there was ⁶ _____ very interesting information about it, too. There weren't ⁷ _____ postcards in the museum shop, but there was ⁸ _____ interesting little book, so I bought you that! Hope you like it!

Speak soon,
Tom

5 ⭐⭐ **Look at the two museum displays and complete the texts with *there was(n't)*/ *there were(n't)*, *a*, *an*, *some* or *any*.**

Home	News	Blog	Lifestyle	

¹ __There was__ an interesting display with objects from a Roman kitchen at our local museum. ² _____ some wooden bowls and ³ _____ knives and forks, but there weren't ⁴ _____ spoons. There was ⁵ _____ metal water bottle. There was also ⁶ _____ very old bread – over a thousand years old, in fact. Yummy!

My favourite display had lovely objects from a woman's bedroom. There was ⁷ _____ old mirror and ⁸ _____ gold jewellery. She was probably ⁹ _____ important person. ¹⁰ _____ a beautiful necklace and a bracelet too, but ¹¹ _____ any earrings. And there was a comb with ¹² _____ human hair in it!

WRITING
A fictional account of a journey

1 ⭐ Read the account and (circle) the best title.

a Swedish family lost in Edale

b Help for teenage walkers in Sweden

c Safe return for lost walkers

Three Swedish teenagers decided to do a famous long-distance walk from England to Scotland. ¹ *They set off on* 22 October, 2018 from Edale, a small village in the English hills.

The walk is 412 km long, and Lucas, Sven and Lilly wanted to complete it in three weeks. They wore big boots and carried heavy bags with their camping equipment. ² _____ it was warm and sunny, but after two days, everything changed. ³ _____ cold and rainy. The walkers' boots got wet and their bags got heavier.

The three friends didn't stop, but ⁴ _____ with the weather. On day four, it became foggy. The path was difficult to see and they got lost. Then Sven fell and broke his leg. There was no one to help them and no mobile phone signal.

⁵ _____ on 27 October, a mountain rescue team found the friends, and they arrived home safely the next day. Now they are planning to do the walk again in the spring.

2 ⭐⭐ Complete the account with the words and phrases in the box.

> At first,   Finally,   The weather was
> there were a lot of problems   ~~They set off on~~

3 ⭐ (Circle) the correct options.

1 The teenagers wanted to walk from *Scotland to England / England to Scotland*.

2 They hoped to do the walk in three *weeks / days*.

3 The weather was *good / bad* on the first two days.

4 *Lucas / Sven* had an accident.

4 ⭐ Match 1–6 with a–f.

1 22 October, 2018 — `b`

2 412 km — ☐

3 after two days — ☐

4 the three friends — ☐

5 28 October, 2018 — ☐

6 in the spring — ☐

a the day they arrived home

b the day they set off

c Lucas, Sven and Lilly

d the length of the walk

e when the friends plan to start again

f the weather changed

Write a fictional account of a journey.

PLAN

5 ⭐⭐ Make notes about the information you need for each paragraph.

1 Who made the journey: _____

_____

When and where it started: _____

_____

Where they planned to go: _____

_____

2 The first part of the journey: _____

_____

The weather: _____

3 How the journey continued: _____

_____

Any problems: _____

_____

4 The end of the journey: _____

_____

WRITE

6 ⭐⭐⭐ Write your fictional account. Remember to include the past simple, *there was/there were* and phrases from the *Useful language* box (see Student's Book, p29).

CHECK

7 Do you ...

• have four paragraphs?

• use the correct language to talk about the past?

• explain what the journey was like?

VOCABULARY

1 **Complete the sentences with weather words. Use the first letter to help you.**

1 When it's f_____ , it's difficult to see where you're going.

2 It's going to be r_____ , so don't forget your umbrella.

3 She wore a hoodie, a scarf and gloves because it was very c_____ .

4 Don't run outside. It's i_____ and you can easily fall.

5 The weather was nice and w_____ . We could swim every day.

6 A branch of the old tree broke on a very s_____ night.

7 It's still c_____ now, but it isn't raining any more.

8 They could eat in the garden because the weather was d_____ .

9 The sun was really h_____ for Sally, so she went inside.

10 I love winter evenings when it's s_____ outside.

11 One horrible w_____ and w_____ night, the rain blew into our tent.

12 Take your sunglasses because it's very s_____ today.

2 **Match the descriptions with the words in the box.**

> blanket   bowl   comb   cup   fork   hairbrush
> lamp   mirror   pillow   plate   scissors
> spoon   toothbrush

1 You can use these to cut hair or paper. _____

2 This helps you to see when it's dark. _____

3 Two objects you use for your hair. _____

4 You need this to clean your teeth. _____

5 Two useful objects you use to put food in your mouth.

   _____ _____

6 You use this at night to keep warm. _____

7 You put soup in a _____ and a sandwich on a

   _____ .

8 You put your tea or coffee in this. _____

9 Your head is on this when you're sleeping in bed.

   _____

10 You look into this when you're combing your hair.

   _____

LANGUAGE IN ACTION

3 **Choose the correct verbs. Then write the past simple form of the verb.**

Vasco da Gama, a Portuguese sailor and explorer, [1](work / arrive) _____worked_____ on the king's ships from 1492. In July 1497, he [2](leave / set) _____ off on a journey to India. He [3](want / become) _____ to find a route to the Far East. He [4](take / travel) _____ a total of 38,600 km. The journey [5](be / go) _____ dangerous and the weather [6](like / be) _____ often stormy. Da Gama [7](take / carry) _____ 170 men with him, but only 54 [8](arrive / stay) _____ home safely in 1499.

4 Complete the sentences with the correct form of *there was/there were* and *a, an, some* or *any*.

1   _There weren't any_ mirrors in the bathroom. (–)
2   _____ information about Egyptian mummies?
3   _____ interesting books in the museum shop. (+)
4   _____ article about dinosaurs in the newspaper. (+)
5   _____ good exhibitions in Berlin?
6   _____ clear answer to my question. (–)
7   _____ bowls in the kitchen. (–)
8   _____ visitors from Portugal in our school. (+)

CUMULATIVE LANGUAGE

5 Complete the conversation with the missing words. (Circle) the correct options.

SARA   Hi, Katie. What ¹_____ at the moment?

KATIE   I'm working really ²_____! I need some ideas for my history project.

SARA   ³_____ the documentary about English kings and queens last Saturday?

KATIE   No, I ⁴_____ camping last weekend, so I missed it.

SARA   That's a shame. It was very ⁵_____.

KATIE   ⁶_____ information about the clothes they wore in the past?

SARA   Yes, and ⁷_____ interesting facts about jewellery. I ⁸_____ about how they made gold and silver artefacts for my history project.

KATIE   I know! I can write about everyday objects in the 16th century.

SARA   ⁹_____ exhibition in the city library last month called 'At Home in the Past'.

KATIE   Really?

SARA   And ¹⁰_____ presentation by a famous history professor.

KATIE   Oh, dear. I ¹¹_____ that, too. I really am a terrible student!

SARA   Don't worry. I ¹²_____ to that presentation, so I can help you.

KATIE   Really? You're a great friend. Thanks, Sara!

1   a do you   b did you do   c are you doing
2   a hardly   b hard   c harder
3   a Saw you   b Did you saw   c Did you see
4   a went   b go   c didn't go
5   a well   b good   c better
6   a Was there any   b Were there any   c Was there an
7   a was there some b weren't there any c there were some
8   a write   b 'm writting   c 'm writing
9   a There's an   b There was an   c There was a
10 a there was a   b was there a   c there was an
11 a was missing   b misses   c missed
12 a go   b went   c going

3 WHAT'S THE STORY?

VOCABULARY
Adjectives of feeling

1 ⭐ **Read the clues and complete the puzzle. Then complete sentence 11 with your own idea.**

```
 1                 11
 L  O  N       E   L  Y
               M
             2 B
             3 A
 4           R
 5           R
             6 A
             7 S
 8           S
             9 E
10           D
```

1 I feel … when I have nobody to talk to.
2 When you have nothing to do, you get … .
3 I don't like big spiders and I feel … when I see one.
4 Before an important test or exam, you can feel … .
5 My parents sometimes get … when I arrive home late.
6 Do your teachers get … when you don't listen to them?
7 I was … to see my friend because she arrived a day early!
8 They were very … when they heard your sad news.
9 Little children get … about their birthdays.
10 You look … . Why don't you go to bed?
11 You feel embarrassed when _____
   _____ .

2 ⭐ **Circle the correct options.**

1 Leave the light on when you feel (afraid) / angry in the dark.
2 Was your brother excited / angry when you took his tablet?
3 Call a friend when you feel tired / lonely and want some company.
4 I'm never excited / bored; there's always something to do.
5 Julio was embarrassed / lonely because he didn't remember my name.

3 ⭐⭐ **Complete the email with the words in the box.**

excited   nervous   ~~surprised~~   tired   upset

● ● ●

| TO: Diana | FROM: Kylie |

Hi Diana,

How are you? I was
¹ _surprised_ when you weren't in class today. Are you
² _____ about the exam tomorrow? I can't revise any more tonight, I'm very
³ _____ – I need to go to bed. My parents get
⁴ _____ when I work late – they think I need more sleep! Don't worry about tomorrow. Just remember our camping trip when the exams are over – I'm ⁵ _____ about that!

See you, Kylie

4 ⭐⭐⭐ **Complete the sentences so they are true for you. Write them in your notebook.**

I feel nervous when … .   I don't get upset when … .
I sometimes feel lonely when … .

Explore it! 👆

Guess the correct answer.

If you have hippophilia, you love hippos / spiders / horses and they make you feel good.

Find another unusual thing that makes people feel good. Then send a question in an email to a classmate or ask them it in the next class.

READING
A folk tale

1 ⭐ **Read the folk tale and match the names (1–3) with the people (a–c).**

1 Manata ⬜   a the young man
2 Matakauri ⬜   b the terrible giant
3 Matau ⬜   c the beautiful girl

The story of Lake Wakatipu

The Māori people of New Zealand have different stories about their country and how it began. One popular Māori story is about Lake Wakatipu. This lake is in the shape of the letter 'S' and there are high mountains all around it.

The story is about the beautiful daughter of a Māori chief. Her name was Manata, and she loved a young man called Matakauri. They wanted to get married, but Manata's father said no because Matakauri was not important. One day, a terrible giant called Matau came down from the mountains and took Manata. Her father was very upset and worried. 'The man who rescues Manata can ask her to marry him,' he said. Many men were afraid of the giant because he was very strong and dangerous. But Matakauri's love for Manata was strong too, so he rescued her and she became his wife.

However, Matakauri was unhappy because the giant was still alive. One winter day, he went back to the giant's home. Matau was sleeping on a bed of dry leaves, when Matakauri started a fire under him. Soon Matau's body was burning, although his heart was still beating. The giant's dead body made a big hole in the ground, in the shape of the letter 'S'. The snow on the mountains melted because of the fire and ran into the hole. This created Lake Wakatipu.

Today, people still tell this story. The water in the lake goes up and down, and people say it is the beating heart of the dead giant!

2 ⭐⭐ **Read the folk tale again and check the meaning of the words in the box in a dictionary. Then complete the sentences.**

> beat ~~burn~~ chief
> giant melt rescue

1 Cook the vegetables on a low heat. Don't _____burn_____ them!

2 The _____ was the most important person in the village.

3 Ice creams _____ in the hot sun.

4 Heroes _____ people from dangerous situations.

5 Does your heart _____ faster when you're excited or nervous?

6 The _____ in the folk tale was ten metres tall!

3 ⭐⭐ **Are the sentences _T_ (true) or _F_ (false)?**

1 Manata's father wasn't an important person. _F_

2 Matakauri wasn't a chief. ___

3 Matakauri and Manata got married after the giant died. ___

4 Matau died in the water when the snow melted. ___

5 Matau's body made a big hole that looked like a letter. ___

6 People tell the story to explain why the water in Lake Wakatipu moves.

4 ⭐⭐⭐ **Choose from the options and complete the sentences in your notebook so they are true for you.**

1 I _think / don't think_ Matakauri was an important person because … .

2 I _like / don't like_ the ending of this story because … .

3 I _believe / don't believe_ folk tales are just for little children because … .

LANGUAGE IN ACTION

Past continuous: affirmative and negative

1 ⭐ **Complete the sentences with the past continuous form of the verbs in brackets.**

1 I _was working_ (work) all afternoon yesterday.

2 Yolanda _____ (make) sandwiches for our picnic.

3 My brother _____ (not sleep) in front of the TV.

4 We _____ (sit) in the car.

5 Clara _____ (look) for her phone.

6 They _____ (not shop) this morning.

2 ⭐⭐ **Look at the photos and correct the sentences. Use the past continuous.**

1 She was playing football.

She wasn't playing football. She was playing tennis.

2 They were texting.

_____

_____

3 He was sleeping.

_____

_____

4 We were sitting on the bus.

_____

_____

3 ⭐⭐ **Complete the email with the past continuous form of the verbs in the box.**

| feel | ~~have~~ | jump | listen | not dance | play | sleep |

Hi Irina,

Happy New Year! I hope you [1] _were having_ fun at midnight last night. I was at a party, and a DJ [2] _____ my favourite songs. I [3] _____ to the music, but I [4] _____ – I [5] _____ really tired. :(My friends [6] _____ up and down on the dance floor all night, though! What about you? Don't tell me that you [7] _____ ! :)

Write back soon!

Jessie

4 ⭐⭐⭐ **Look at the picture and complete the story with suitable verbs in the past continuous. There may be more than one possibility.**

I had an interesting dream last night. I [1] _was sitting_ in a winter garden. Everything was white because it [2] _____, and I was very cold because I [3] _____ winter clothes. A big brown bear [4] _____ in front of me on two legs. It was very tall! It looked angry and dangerous. I don't know why, but I [5] _____ afraid at all. I [6] _____ nicely to the bear in a very friendly voice, but the bear [7] _____ to me! Then suddenly the bear [8] _____ a guitar and singing! In the end, I started to get angry with the bear. Then I woke up!

VOCABULARY AND LISTENING

Prepositions of movement

1 ⭐ **Complete the prepositions with the missing vowels.**

1 u n d e r
2 _ p
3 _ c r _ s s
4 p _ s t
5 _ _ t _ f
6 t h r _ _ g h

7 _ n t _
8 b _ t w _ _ n
9 d _ w n
10 _ l _ n g
11 _ v _ r
12 _ f f

2 ⭐⭐ **Complete the sentences with the prepositions in the box.**

> ~~along~~ into off over through under

1 I was walking ___along___ the river yesterday afternoon.
2 They were having a picnic _____ the trees.
3 Our dog was running after a cat, but it jumped _____ the wall.
4 When she lost her keys, she climbed into her house _____ the open window.
5 We can get _____ the bus here and walk to my house.
6 Mum walked _____ the shop and asked the assistant for help.

3 ⭐⭐ **Look at the photos and complete the sentences with prepositions from Exercise 1.**

1 He was running ___down___ the stairs.
2 Shelia was getting _____ the taxi.
3 The sisters were walking _____ their parents.
4 Jodie was going _____ the table.
5 Dominic was jumping _____ the water.
6 Dan was walking _____ the street.

A radio phone-in

4 ⭐ **Look at the picture. What do you think the story is about? Predict the words you might hear.**

_____

🎧 5 ⭐ **Listen to Bruno's story. Do you hear any of your words from Exercise 4?**
3.01

🎧 6 ⭐⭐ **Listen again and (circle) the correct answers.**
3.01

1 The radio programme is about … things that happen to people.
  a dangerous (b) funny
  c embarrassing
2 When Bruno got off the bus, a man was running … .
  a across the road   b into a bank
  c out of a bank
3 The man had a … .
  a knife in a bag   b knife   c bag
4 The alarm bells were ringing … .
  a in the bus   b inside the bank
  c outside the bank
5 The people at the bus stop were … .
  a helping the man
  b not doing anything
  c helping the policeman
6 The policeman caught the man because … stopped him.
  a a woman   b Bruno   c some dogs

7 ⭐⭐⭐ **Answer the questions.**

1 How do you think the people at the bus stop felt?

_____

2 Did they do the right thing? Why / Why not?

_____

LANGUAGE IN ACTION
Past continuous: questions

1 ⭐ **Put the words in the correct order to make past continuous questions.**

1 you / watching / night / Were / last / news / the / ?

  <u>Were you watching the news last night?</u>

2 the / long / a / wearing / woman / coat / Was / ?

  _____

3 along / Were / road / your / skating / friends / the / ?

  _____

4 through / people / many / park / were / How / the / walking / ?

  _____

5 into / Where / children / river / were / the / the / jumping / ?

  _____

6 off / bus / the / passengers / were / Why / the / getting / ?

  _____

2 ⭐⭐ **Write past continuous questions and short answers about the story in Exercise 5 on page 27.**

1 A the man / wear / a hoodie / ?

  <u>Was the man wearing a hoodie?</u>

  B <u>No, he wasn't.</u>

2 A he / carry / a black bag / ?

  B _____

3 A alarm bells / ring / in the bank / ?

  B _____

4 A the policeman / ride / a motorbike / ?

  B _____

5 A the people / help / the policeman / ?

  B _____

6 A the dogs / run after / the man / ?

  B _____

Past simple and past continuous

3 ⭐⭐ Ⓒircle **the correct options.**

1 Our neighbour (fell) / was falling while he walked / (was walking) into the town.

2 While she looked / was looking for her bag, she found / was finding an old photo.

3 William didn't hear / wasn't hearing the man when he stood / was standing behind him.

4 We cycled / were cycling home when the storm started / was starting.

5 She had / was having a problem when she did / was doing her homework.

6 Did they sit / Were they sitting on the bus when it hit / was hitting the car?

4 ⭐⭐ <u>Underline</u> **and correct one mistake in each sentence.**

1 Ann was doing her homework <u>while</u> her mother came into her room. _____when_____

2 My friend was looking at her phone as the teacher saw her. _____

3 While we were eating dinner, the cat was jumping onto the table and surprised us! _____

4 He was playing rugby when he was breaking his leg. _____

5 Weren't you answering the phone when it rang?

  _____

5 ⭐⭐ **Complete the text with the past simple or past continuous form of the verbs in the box.**

leave	not look	not see	play
stand	steal	take	~~wait~~	walk

Caught on camera!

I ¹ <u>was waiting</u> for a friend in the park. I ² _____ under a small tree – that's why the girl ³ _____ me. She ⁴ _____ across the park quickly to where a man ⁵ _____ football with his son. The man's backpack was under a chair, and the girl ⁶ _____ it when he ⁷ _____ in her direction. As the girl ⁸ _____ the park, I ⁹ _____ a photo of her.

WRITING
A story

1 ⭐ **Look at the notes. What do you think Olive's story is about? Read the story and check your ideas.**

A misunderstanding
By Olive Crooke

One day last summer, I was playing tennis with some friends after school and I got home late. At first, I thought my parents were working, but then I noticed the car wasn't outside. There was no one in the house. Then I remembered they were all shopping.

A few minutes later, I went to get a snack, and I saw a note on the fridge from my dad. It said, 'We were waiting for you, but it got late. Your dinner's in the fridge. Back soon.' I found a bowl of food and took it out. It didn't look very nice, but I was hungry, so I started to eat it. Suddenly, I saw another note on the table from my mum. It said, 'Please feed the cat – her food's in a bowl in the fridge.' I was eating the cat's dinner!

In the end, I didn't feel well, so the next morning I didn't go to school. My brothers thought it was very funny, but I wasn't laughing!

2 ⭐⭐ **Read the story again. Are the sentences *T* (true) or *F* (false)?**

1 Olive's story happened in the spring. F
2 Her parents were at work. ___
3 Olive's parents wanted her to go shopping with them. ___
4 She stayed at home the day after eating the cat food. ___
5 She thought it was a funny accident. ___

3 ⭐⭐ **Read the story again and put the events (a–g) in the correct order (1–7).**

a She didn't go to school the next day. ☐
b Olive was playing tennis. ☐1
c She found a note about her dinner. ☐
d She saw a note about the cat's dinner. ☐
e She found a bowl of food and started eating it. ☐
f She came home late and the house was empty. ☐
g She realised her mistake and felt ill. ☐

4 ⭐⭐ **Put the phrases in the order they appear in the story.**

a A few minutes later, ☐
b In the end, ☐
c Suddenly, ☐
d At first, ☐
e the next morning ☐
f One day last summer, ☐1

Write a story.
PLAN
5 ⭐⭐ **Think about a misunderstanding that happened to you, or invent one. Make notes about these things.**

1 What was happening before the main events started: _____

  What happened first: _____

2 The main events of the story: _____

3 What happened in the end: _____

WRITE
6 ⭐⭐⭐ **Write your story. Remember to include three paragraphs, the past simple and past continuous, and the vocabulary from this unit.**

CHECK
7 **Do you …**
• use the phrases from the *Useful language* box (see Student's Book, p41)?
• explain the main events?
• explain what happened in the end?

VOCABULARY

1 Complete the sentences with adjectives of feeling. Use the first letter to help you.

1 I'm w_____ about my sister because she isn't feeling very happy.

2 He felt e_____ when he didn't understand the message.

3 Linda is busy all the time! She's never b_____.

4 Don't be n_____ about your exams. You'll be fine.

5 Are you a_____ of cows? They're big and they can get angry!

6 We were s_____ when some old friends from Mexico suddenly came to our door!

7 Sara felt l_____ at first when she moved to the new town. She didn't have any friends.

8 Do your parents get a_____ at you when you come home late?

9 Don't get so e_____! It's only a little birthday present!

10 They were all t_____ after running and doing exercise all day.

11 Don't be u_____ when you don't get 100% in a test. No one gets that!

2 Match 1–6 with a–f.

1 They ran quickly down ☐

2 She was sitting between ☐

3 When you walk past ☐

4 We jumped off the boat ☐

5 Tell the driver your address ☐

6 Look right, left, then right again ☐

a when you get into the taxi.

b into the river.

c her two best friends.

d before you walk across that road.

e my house, you can always come in.

f the stairs and out into the street.

3 Look at the photos and ⟨circle⟩ the correct prepositions.

1 The boat went *across* / *under* the bridge.

2 Kim was running *along* / *across* the road.

3 He jumped *through* / *over* the wall.

4 The cat came *through* / *under* the kitchen window.

5 The movie star got *out of* / *into* the car.

6 Lena climbed *over* / *up* a tree.

LANGUAGE IN ACTION

4 Complete the email with the past continuous form of the verbs in the box.

> discuss   laugh   sing   talk   think

● ● ●

Dear Danny,

I'm sorry you were upset earlier today in music class. I'm embarrassed because when you were about to sing, Eva and I ¹_____ to each other quite loudly. Then you ²_____ really well and we ³_____, but only because it was a funny song. Anyway, at a meeting yesterday, we ⁴_____ our band. We decided we need a lead singer and, of course, all the time we ⁵_____ of you. Would you like to be our singer? Please say 'yes'!

Emily

5 Write past continuous questions for the answers.

1 Why _____ ?

She was feeling nervous because she had an exam.

2 What _____ ?

They were talking about their new project.

3 Who _____ ?

He was visiting his grandparents.

4 Where _____ ?

I was camping in France.

5 Why _____ ?

We were running because we were late.

6 How long _____ ?

She was waiting for more than an hour.

6 Complete the sentences with the past simple or past continuous form of the verbs in brackets.

1 While we _____ (wait) for our friends, we _____ (start) to make tea.

2 He _____ (hear) the good news while he _____ (sit) on the train.

3 Someone _____ (call) you while you _____ (have) a shower.

4 When their parents _____ (return), a band _____ (play) in their garage.

5 When the film _____ (finish), everyone in the cinema _____ (cry).

6 While I _____ (look) for my shoes, I _____ (find) an old sandwich under my bed.

CUMULATIVE LANGUAGE

7 Complete the conversation with the missing words. Circle the correct options.

JAKE   Hi, Bella! Are you OK? When I ¹_____ you yesterday, you were looking upset.

BELLA   There were ²_____ problems at home.

JAKE   That's ³_____ . What were you doing? Did you have a lot of homework?

BELLA   No, I ⁴_____ . But I was angry with my little brother.

JAKE   Really? What ⁵_____ ?

BELLA   Oh, he ⁶_____ horrible noisy video games all evening.

JAKE   My sister ⁷_____ playing those, too. What was the problem?

BELLA   Well, he was making a terrible noise while I ⁸_____ my favourite show.

JAKE   Come on, Bella. Sometimes it can be difficult to play video games ⁹_____ .

BELLA   I never ¹⁰_____ video games!

JAKE   OK, so what ¹¹_____ in the end?

BELLA   Well, in the end I ¹²_____ Billy's tablet and hid it in a very secret place … in the kitchen.

JAKE   You're kidding!

1	a	seeing	b	was seeing	c saw
2	a	any	b	some	c a
3	a	bad	b	well	c badly
4	a	did	b	do	c didn't
5	a	did he do	b	did he	c he did
6	a	plays	b	playing	c was playing
7	a	loves	b	is loving	c doesn't love
8	a	watch	b	was watching	c watched
9	a	quietly	b	quieter	c quiet
10	a	am playing	b	to play	c play
11	a	happened	b	was happening	c happens
12	a	was taking	b	take	c took

4 THE BEST THINGS IN LIFE ARE FREE

VOCABULARY
Money verbs

1 ⭐ **Put the letters in the correct order to make money verbs.**

1 s o t c _____cost_____

2 n e h g c a _____

3 r n a e _____

4 r o o r w b _____

5 e p n d s _____

6 l e s l _____

7 y a p _____

8 d l n e _____

9 v a e s _____

10 e o w _____

2 ⭐ (Circle) **the correct options.**

1 (Save) / Spend your money for something you really want.

2 Please can you borrow / lend me £5?

3 How much did that phone sell / cost you?

4 Harry earns / spends £2.50 when he washes his mum's car.

5 I don't like changing / owing my friends money.

6 She sold / bought her old bike to a school friend.

3 ⭐ **Complete the sentences with the words in the box.**

| change   cost   ~~earn~~   pay   sell   spend |

1 You ___earn___ money for work you do.

2 How much did those cool trainers _____?

3 Can we _____ for our drinks with euros on the plane?

4 Supermarkets _____ many different things to their customers.

5 Where can I _____ my Brazilian reals into pounds?

6 Don't _____ all your birthday money on video games and sweets!

4 ⭐⭐ **Complete the text messages with money verbs from Exercise 1.**

I can't ¹_____pay_____ for my phone this month. Can I ²_____ £10 from you, please?

But you ³_____ me £5 from last month! ☹ I can't ⁴_____ you any more. Sorry.

What can I do? It's impossible to ⁵_____ money – I never have any left at the end of the week.

You can ⁶_____ me your skateboard for £15. 😊

My skateboard ⁷_____ £50 when I bought it!

Oh, well. Sorry, I can't help you then.

5 ⭐⭐ **Complete the definitions with the correct form of the similar words in each pair.**

1 You ___lend___ some money to a friend. Your friend _____ money from you. (borrow / lend)

2 A shop assistant _____ something to you. You _____ something from a shop assistant. (buy / sell)

3 People _____ money for things they need. They _____ money in a shop or online. (save / spend)

4 You _____ money when you work. You _____ money in a competition or a lottery. (earn / win)

Explore it! 🖱

True or false?

In the USA, they print more Monopoly money than real dollars every year.

Find an interesting fact about banknotes or coins. Then send a question in an email to a classmate or ask them it in the next class.

READING
A newspaper article

1 ⭐ Read the article. Which opinion in the last paragraph do you agree with? _____

Goodbye to Saturday jobs?

Fifty years ago, it was very common for a British teenager to work part-time. These days, the number of teens with a 'Saturday job' is falling.

The most common jobs in the UK for young people are delivering newspapers and working in shops and offices, or as waiters. In the past, teens could easily get these jobs. Now, employers need special permits for teens under 16 to work in their businesses. Also, 13 to 15-year-olds can't work between the hours of 7 pm and 7 am.

Another reason for the fall in part-time teenage workers is that in the past they could have a part-time job and do their schoolwork. Now, success in exams is the most important thing, and there's more pressure to do well at school.

'Working part-time and doing well at school isn't easy,' says 15-year-old shop assistant Cheryl Bates. 'You need to organise your time and maybe do some of your homework at lunchtime. It's harder than you think, but when I earn my own money, I feel more independent because I don't need to ask my parents to buy me things.'

Fourteen-year-old waiter Martin Cox adds, 'Doing a job is the best way to

learn the skills you need for the future. I was the quietest boy in my class, and I couldn't talk to people very well. Now, because I talk to customers at work, I'm much better in social situations.'

So, can part-time work help to prepare young people for adult life, or does it put extra pressure on teens with already busy lives? What do you think?

2 ⭐⭐ Read the article again and check the meaning of the words in the box in a dictionary. Then complete the sentences.

> common   employer   ~~independent~~
> part-time   permit   pressure

1 Maisie is a very _independent_ girl. She never needs much help.
2 Is there much _____ to pass all your exams at your school?
3 Fruit picking is usually a _____ job in the summer months. It's a very _____ job in lots of countries.
4 Mrs Preston is a good _____. All her teenage workers really like her.
5 Do you need a _____ to work here when you're under 16?

3 ⭐⭐ Read the article again. Are the sentences *T* (true) or *F* (false)?

1 In the UK, there weren't many young part-time workers in the past. _F_
2 A 16-year-old girl can work in a shop without a permit. ____
3 A 14-year-old boy can work between 7 am and 7 pm. ____
4 There was more pressure to do well at school in the past. ____
5 Cheryl thinks earning her own money is easy. ____
6 For Martin, talking to people isn't a problem now. ____

4 ⭐⭐⭐ Answer the questions with your own ideas.

1 Is part-time work for teenagers common in your country? Why / Why not?
_____
_____
2 How do you get the money to buy the things you want?
_____

LANGUAGE IN ACTION
could

1 ⭐ **Match 1–6 with a–f.**

1 I had no money, ☐ e
2 Sara couldn't lend me £10 ☐
3 All the lights in the shop went out ☐
4 Mozart could play and write music ☐
5 My dad could run marathons ☐
6 The bank was closed, ☐

a because she didn't have any money.
b so they couldn't change their dollars.
c from the age of four.
d and we couldn't see anything.
e so I couldn't buy anything.
f when he was younger.

2 ⭐⭐ **Write sentences that are true for you when you were six. Use the pictures.**

One, two, three … eight, nine, ten

100 metres

1 When I was six, I couldn't ride a bike.
2 _____
3 _____
4 _____
5 _____
6 _____

Comparative and superlative adjectives

3 ⭐ **Circle the correct options.**

1 The film was (more exciting) / *the most exciting* than the book.
2 Samir was *happier* / *the happiest* in his old job than he is now.
3 Money isn't *more important* / *the most important* thing in life.
4 It was *more difficult* / *the most difficult* decision for him to make.
5 Today's lesson was *shorter* / *the shortest* than yesterday's.
6 The shop assistants were *more helpful* / *the most helpful* than they usually are.

4 ⭐⭐ **Put the words in the correct order to make sentences.**

1 yesterday / than / was / It's / today / it / hotter
   It's hotter today than it was yesterday.
2 mine / phone / than / your / Was / expensive / more / ?
   _____
3 worse / What's / than / your / losing / wallet / ?
   _____
4 quietest / town / Monday / the / is / in / day
   _____
5 are / cheapest / shop / the / jeans / These / in / the
   _____
6 best / life / Yesterday / of / the / my / day / was
   _____

5 ⭐⭐ **Complete the text with the comparative or superlative form of the adjectives in the box.**

> exciting expensive ~~famous~~ old rich successful

I got some money for my birthday, so I bought a ticket to a City game. Everyone knows City: they're [1] the most famous football team in the world. I think they're [2] _____ than the other clubs in my country because my great-grandad was a City fan when he was a kid, and that was a long time ago! And they've got lots of money, so they're definitely [3] _____ . Their football is fast and they score lots of goals, so they're [4] _____ to watch than other teams. I also think they are [5] _____ team because they win most of their games. The only bad thing is I can't go to every match because the tickets are probably [6] _____ tickets in the world.

VOCABULARY AND LISTENING

Caring jobs

1 ⭐ **Complete the crossword. Use the clues.**

Across

1 A … helps old or sick people in their homes.
3 A … gives advice to people about the law.
7 A … helps to protect people from crime.
8 A … cares for sick people in hospitals.
9 A … works for no money.

Down

1 A … works in organisations like Oxfam and WaterAid.
2 A … gives medical help to people before they get to hospital.
4 A … does operations in hospitals.
5 A … rescues people from dangerous situations.
6 A … looks after swimmers.
9 A … is a doctor for animals.

Put the grey letters in the correct order to complete this clue: A _____
takes away the things we don't want.

2 ⭐ (Circle) the correct options.

1 The (lifeguard) / firefighter told us not to swim.
2 When a car hit our dog, we took it to the vet / lawyer.
3 The paramedic / police officer stopped the motorbike because it was going very fast.
4 The firefighter / refuse collector climbed into the burning house through a window.
5 My neighbour is a vet / carer in an old people's home.

Monologues

🎧 **3** ⭐ **Listen to three people talking about their jobs. Which place connects all three speakers?** _____
4.01

🎧 **4** ⭐⭐ **Listen again and** (circle) **the correct answers.**
4.01

1 Speaker 1 …
   a never has time for her family.
   (b) spent a long time studying.
   c doesn't spend much time working.

2 Speaker 1 …
   a needs a lot of help from her team.
   b prefers working alone.
   c thinks the nurses need to work harder.

3 Speaker 2 …
   a thinks his job is more important than a doctor's job.
   b didn't want to be a nurse when he was younger.
   c is doing the work he always wanted to do.

4 Speaker 2 thinks …
   a some nurses are leaving because the job isn't well paid.
   b it's sad that nurses want more money.
   c nurses need more responsibilities.

5 Speaker 3 does her job …
   a at the weekend.   b in the morning.
   c three days a week.

5 ⭐⭐⭐ **Answer the questions in your notebook.**

1 Which job is the most tiring? Why?
2 Which job is the most important? Why?

LANGUAGE IN ACTION
too, too much, too many

1 ⭐ **Complete the sentences with *too* and the words in the box.**

> busy   expensive   hard   hot   ~~tired~~   young

1 The nurses were ___too tired___ to go out after work.
2 The hospital car park costs £10. That's _____ .
3 Is John _____ to stop working as a firefighter?
4 It was _____ in the sun, so I went inside.
5 Can you help me this morning or are you _____ ?
6 They couldn't answer the question because it was _____ .

2 ⭐ Ⓒircle the correct options.

1 The doctor gave us too ⓜuch / *many* information when she called.
2 Were there too *much* / *many* people in the waiting room?
3 Most carers say that they have too *much* / *many* work.
4 Don't put too *much* / *many* milk in my coffee, please.
5 Is it possible to have too *much* / *many* good ideas?
6 Do you think surgeons earn too *much* / *many* money?

3 ⭐⭐ **Complete the conversation with *too*, *too much* or *too many*.**

CHRIS What a day! I've got [1] ___too many___ children in my class.

LILY Me too. Over 30 in my group and they've all got [2] _____ energy. It gets [3] _____ noisy sometimes!

CHRIS True! And they say we give them [4] _____ homework, and that it's [5] _____ difficult.

LILY I know, but it's difficult for us, too – there are always [6] _____ notebooks for us to look at!

(not) enough + noun

4 ⭐⭐ **Put the words in the correct order to make sentences.**

1 enough / don't / Doctors / money / nurses / and / earn
   Doctors and nurses don't earn enough money.
2 food / everyone / the / There / for / enough / is / in / world
   _____
3 volunteers / Are / organisation / enough / your / in / there / ?
   _____
4 moment / enough / We / at / information / got / haven't / the
   _____
5 in / Is / enough / classroom / space / this / there / ?
   _____

5 ⭐⭐ **Underline and correct one mistake in each sentence.**

1 Footballers earn too <u>many</u> money, in my opinion. ____much____
2 It's too noise in here for me; please be quiet. _____
3 The teacher gave us too much options to think about. _____
4 There wasn't information enough on the poster. _____
5 She was much young to volunteer for a caring job. _____

6 ⭐⭐ **Complete the text about a dream job with *too*, *too much*, *too many* or (*not*) *enough*.**

My dream job is to be a paramedic. Everyone knows that there are [1] ___n't enough___ doctors, but [2] _____ people forget about the paramedics. I don't want to spend [3] _____ time studying when I finish school and you don't need to take [4] _____ exams in emergency medicine to do it. But of course, you need to take some exams and you need to be a good driver. When the roads are [5] _____ full of cars, you need [6] _____ driving skills to get to the hospital safely and quickly!

WRITING
An opinion essay

1 ⭐ **Read David's essay. Does he agree with the statement?**

It's good to have a Saturday job while you're still at school. Do you agree?
By David Rodríguez

1 Nowadays, things cost a lot and you need enough money to buy them. With a Saturday job you can earn your own money, but ¹ ___in my opinion___ , it's not a good idea.

2 ² _____ , working in a supermarket or café can sometimes be boring. Also, a student often gets lower pay than an adult for the same type of job. Perhaps because of this, more students get these jobs, and there isn't enough work for older people with families who need money more than you.

3 Also, teenagers usually sleep longer and get up later on Saturdays. ³ _____ that when you study hard at school all week, you need to relax at the weekend. I also think that enjoying free-time activities is more important than earning money.

4 ⁴ _____ , students need enough time for schoolwork, relaxing and doing free-time activities. ⁵ _____ it's better to rest at the weekend and spend more time doing your favourite things. We'll have enough time for work when we're older!

2 ⭐ **Complete the essay with the phrases in the box.**

> First of all   I believe that   ~~in my opinion~~
> Personally, I think   To sum up

3 ⭐⭐ **Read the essay again and answer the questions.**

1 What examples of part-time jobs does David give?

_____

2 In David's opinion, why can part-time jobs for teens be a problem for adults?

_____

3 According to David, what do teenagers typically do on Saturday mornings?

_____

4 What does David say is more important than money?

_____

4 ⭐ **Match the paragraphs (1–4) with the summaries (a–d).**

a a first reason for your opinion ☐

b a summary of your opinion ☐

c an introduction to the topic and your opinion ☐

d a second reason for your opinion ☐

Write an opinion essay.

PLAN

5 ⭐⭐ **Choose one of the following topics or use David's topic. Make notes about the information you need for each paragraph.**

• Saturday jobs teach you the skills you need for the future.

• Hard-working teachers don't earn enough money.

1 Introduce the topic and give your opinion:

_____

2 Give a reason for your opinion:

_____

3 Give a second reason:

_____

4 Summarise your opinion:

_____

WRITE

6 ⭐⭐⭐ **Write your opinion essay. Remember to include (*not*) *enough* and *too*, *too much*, *too many*, and the phrases from the *Useful language* box (see Student's Book, p53).**

CHECK

7 Do you …

• have four paragraphs?

• give reasons for your opinions?

• summarise your opinion at the end?

VOCABULARY

1 Match 1–8 with a–h.

1 Henry lent his sister ☐
2 How much did you ☐
3 I borrowed £5 more from Ben, ☐
4 You can earn more money ☐
5 Are you saving money ☐
6 Do they sell ☐
7 How much does it cost ☐
8 I spend a lot of money ☐

a for anything special?
b when you work longer hours.
c on presents for my friends.
d to change money here?
e pay for those tickets?
f so now I owe him £10.
g jeans in this sports shop?
h some money for her lunch.

2 Circle the correct options.

1 *charity worker / paramedic*

2 *carer / lifeguard*

3 *vet / lifeguard*

4 *refuse collector / surgeon*

5 *nurse / volunteer*

6 *lawyer / police officer*

LANGUAGE IN ACTION

3 Complete the sentences with *could* or *couldn't*.

1 In the 1970s, people _____ send texts.
2 Roads were safer 50 years ago, so my grandad _____ walk to school.
3 He _____ cycle because he didn't have a bike.
4 My great-grandma _____ play football because it was for boys only in those days.
5 My mum _____ play lots of sports at school. She played tennis, basketball and volleyball.
6 Teenagers in 1950 _____ watch on-demand TV because there wasn't any.

4 Complete the conversation with the comparative or superlative form of the adjectives in brackets.

PABLO Hey, Laura. What's up?

LAURA My exam results were
¹_____ (bad) than last time.

PABLO Oh, dear. And your parents were
²_____ (angry) than usual, right?

LAURA Right. Dad was ³_____ (worried) about them than Mum, but I think I was the ⁴_____ (upset).

PABLO I can understand that. You're the
⁵_____ (hard-working) student in the class.

LAURA Thanks, but I think you're a
⁶_____ (hard) worker than me.

PABLO OK, we both work hard. But doing well in exams is ⁷_____ (difficult) than parents think. It isn't the ⁸_____ (easy) thing in the world!

5 Complete the conversation with *too, too much, too many* or *(not) enough*.

PAT   Can you come swimming today? It's not ¹_____ busy on Sunday mornings.

JAMES Sorry, I can't. I haven't got ²_____ time.

PAT   Really? We don't have ³_____ homework this weekend, only a little bit.

JAMES No, but I've got ⁴_____ jobs to do at home.

PAT   Why do you need to do jobs?

JAMES I don't have ⁵_____ money, so my parents pay me to help with the chores on Sundays.

PAT   Well, I need more money too, but I'm ⁶_____ lazy to do any extra work!

CUMULATIVE LANGUAGE

6 Complete the conversation with the missing words. (Circle) the correct options.

FRAN   Excuse me, I ¹_____ older people for my school magazine. Can you answer a few questions, please?

NIGEL Sure. I hope you haven't got ²_____ difficult questions for me.

FRAN   No, don't worry! The first question is the ³_____ – have you still got a job?

NIGEL Well, I ⁴_____ as a firefighter for many years, but I'm retired now.

FRAN   I see. So now what ⁵_____ every day? Do you like reading or doing sudoku?

NIGEL Certainly not! I've got ⁶_____ energy to sit around all day.

FRAN   You're ⁷_____ my grandparents, then, because that's all they do!

NIGEL Of course I enjoy my free time, but I get ⁸_____ bored when I do nothing.

FRAN   So are there ⁹_____ special things you do, now that you're not working?

NIGEL I'm a volunteer at ¹⁰_____ outdoor activity centre, where I give talks about being safe.

FRAN   That's great! In my opinion, ¹¹_____ retired people share their skills.

NIGEL Very true. It's definitely the ¹²_____ way to stay active and healthy! Next question?

1	a interviewed	b 'm interviewing	c I was interviewing
2	a too much	b too many	c enough
3	a most easy	b easy	c easiest
4	a was work	b working	c worked
5	a do you do	b did you do	c are you doing
6	a much	b enough	c too much
7	a fittest than	b fitter than	c fittest that
8	a too	b too much	c not enough
9	a much	b an	c any
10	a some	b a	c an
11	a not enough	b much	c not much
12	a good	b better	c best

5 DREAM HOUSES

VOCABULARY
Furniture

1 ⭐ Look at the photos and complete the furniture words.

1 a r m c h a i r
2 c _ _ _ _ _ o _
   d _ _ _ _ _ _ _
3 c _ _ _ _ _ _ _ _
4 s _ _ _ _ _ _ _
5 p _ _ _ _ _ _ _
6 b _ _ _ _ _ _ _ _
7 d _ _ _
8 f _ _ _ _ _
9 c _ _ _ _ _ _ _ _
10 w _ _ _ _ _ _ _ _
11 c _ _ _ _ _ _
12 f _ _ _ _ _
13 s _ _ _ _

2 ⭐ (Circle) the correct options to complete the text.

I love my bedroom and spend a lot of time in it. There's a nice warm ¹*cupboard* / (*carpet*) on the ²*floor* / *ceiling* and I've got a comfortable old ³*chest of drawers* / *armchair* by the window, where I can sit and read. In the corner is a ⁴*desk* / *sink* where I do my homework, and above it are some ⁵*shelves* / *pictures* of my friends and family. I've got a big ⁶*fridge* / *wardrobe* for my clothes, but I sometimes leave them on my bed!

3 ⭐⭐ Complete the sentences with words from Exercise 1.

1 Sheila isn't very tall, so she can't touch the ___ceiling___ in her bedroom.
2 Aunt Adie has an old _____ of her grandparents on the wall.
3 He keeps his smaller clothes, like socks and T-shirts, in the _____ .
4 Don't come in with dirty shoes. I washed the kitchen _____ this morning.
5 You can find tea and coffee in that _____ next to the window.
6 We brush our teeth at the _____ in the bathroom.

Explore it! 🖱️

Guess the correct answer.
The biggest hotel in Europe is the Izmailovo Hotel in Moscow. It's got *3,500* / *7,500* / *9,500* beds.

Find another interesting fact about a hotel. Then send a question in an email to a classmate or ask them it in the next class.

READING
A magazine article

1 ⭐⭐ Read the article. In your opinion, which is the best place to live in? _____

No place like home

In this week's edition of *City Life*, we ask two 13-year-olds about living in London. What do they like about where they live? Is there anything they don't like?

'I live in an apartment building in Wembley, in the north-west of London. It's got 21 floors! I live on the second to top floor. City life isn't as quiet as life in the country, but it's very quiet so high up, and the views are amazing. I can see Wembley football stadium from my bedroom window, and I can sometimes hear the crowd when they score a goal! We live near a canal, and I can cycle to school in five minutes along the canal path. It's great to live here. I only think my apartment isn't as good as a house when the lift doesn't work!'

Kelly

'I live in a row of houses in a part of London called Camden. It takes me about ten minutes to walk to school from home. There's a famous market nearby called Camden Lock. It's very popular with street musicians – and tourists, of course! The houses in my street are all painted different colours, but I don't like that very much. I think it's too colourful! My room is at the top of my house. The ceiling isn't as high as I'd like, but the room is big enough for just me. From my window, I can watch the boats and barges go past on the Regent's Canal at the end of our garden. I love living in my house.'

Hasan

2 ⭐⭐ Read the article again and check the meaning of these words in a dictionary. Then complete the sentences.

barge   canal   crowd   ~~floor~~   path   row

1 We stayed on the top _____*floor*_____ of an apartment building in New York.
2 We sat on the front _____ of chairs during the class presentations.
3 My Dutch friend lives on a houseboat on a _____ .
4 A type of boat called a _____ transports things along rivers and canals.
5 To get to the village, follow this _____ .
6 There was a big _____ of people after the car accident.

3 ⭐⭐ (Circle) the correct answers.

1 *City Life* magazine asked Kelly and Hasan about … in London.
  a cycling   b going to school
  (c) living
2 Kelly lives on the … floor.
  a 20th   b 21st   c 2nd
3 She likes … .
  a living high up   b walking to school
  c watching football
4 Hasan's house is in … .
  a a market   b a row
  c Camden Lock
5 He doesn't like the … in his street.
  a tourists   b coloured houses
  c musicians
6 From his bedroom, he can see … .
  a market stalls   b coloured houses
  c boats and barges

4 ⭐⭐⭐ Answer the questions with your own ideas.

1 How are the houses in the article similar to your house?

_____

2 Name one good thing and one bad thing about living in a tall building.

_____

LANGUAGE IN ACTION

(*not*) *as* + *adjective* + *as*

1 ⭐ **Complete the sentences with the adjective in brackets and (*not*) *as … as*. Then check your answers in the article on page 41.**

1 Hasan is ___as happy as___ (happy) Kelly with his home.

2 Kelly thinks country life is _____ (noisy) life in the city.

3 Kelly's journey to school is _____ (slow) Hasan's journey.

4 Hasan is _____ (old) Kelly.

5 The house is _____ (tall) the apartment building.

6 The apartment building is _____ (colourful) the houses in Camden.

2 ⭐⭐ **Look at the information and complete the sentences with *is* (*not*) *as … as* and an adjective from the box.**

> big   busy   ~~expensive~~   fast   good   old

1 Tim's ticket = £10.00 / Liz's ticket = £12.00

   Tim's ticket ___isn't as expensive as___ Liz's ticket.

2 house = 200 metres / apartment = 200 metres

   The apartment _____ the house.

3 Borja's English exam = 8 out of 10 / Olivia's English exam = 8 out of 10

   Olivia's exam result _____ Borja's exam result.

4 Saturday market = 200 shoppers / Monday market = 50 shoppers

   The Monday market _____ the Saturday market.

5 a letter = two days / an email = two seconds

   A letter _____ an email.

6 Luke = 15 years old / Nick = 15 years old

   Luke _____ Nick.

(*not*) + *adjective* + *enough*

3 ⭐ **Complete the sentences with the adjectives in the box.**

> ~~fit~~   hot   old   safe   well

1 I'd love to be ___fit___ enough to run a marathon, but I'm not.

2 See the red flag? The water here isn't _____ enough to swim in.

3 The soup isn't _____ enough. It needs five more minutes.

4 When are you _____ enough to drive a car in your country?

5 He was in hospital and he's still not _____ enough to go to school.

4 ⭐ **Match 1–6 with a–f.**

1 You can take a shower ☐ d

2 This puzzle is too easy ☐

3 Can I have some sugar, please? ☐

4 We didn't understand because ☐

5 He tried to park his car, ☐

6 Her new coat is ☐

a smart enough for the party.

b My coffee isn't sweet enough.

c the instructions weren't clear enough.

d when the water is warm enough.

e because the clues aren't hard enough.

f but the space wasn't wide enough.

5 ⭐⭐ **Complete the conversation with the phrases in the box.**

> as comfortable as   as expensive as   as nice as
> as tall as   ~~long enough~~   soft enough

SARA Here's a furniture shop. Can we look for a new bed for me, Mum? My old bed isn't [1] ___long enough___ for me any more.

MUM I know, you're nearly [2] _____ me now! OK, what about this bed?

SARA Mmm, it isn't [3] _____ for me – it's too hard. It isn't [4] _____ the one I've got now!

MUM Look! This one isn't [5] _____ that one – it's a better price and it's the right size.

SARA But it's not [6] _____ the first one. I'm not sure about the colour. Oh, I can't decide, Mum!

VOCABULARY AND LISTENING Street interviews
Household chores

1 ⭐ (Circle) the correct verbs to complete the household chores.

1 (clean) / *make* the kitchen
2 *make* / *do* the ironing
3 *do* / *make* your bed
4 *empty* / *tidy up* the washing machine
5 *load* / *make* the dishwasher
6 *make* / *do* the washing-up
7 *load* / *tidy up* the living room
8 *empty* / *vacuum* the carpet
9 *do* / *make* the washing

2 ⭐ Match the photos with six of the phrases from Exercise 1.

1   do the ironing

2 _____

3 _____

5 _____

4 _____

6 _____

🎧 **3** ⭐ Listen to an interview about how a family shares the chores at home. Who helps more: Daisy or Milo?
5.01

_____

🎧 **4** ⭐⭐ Listen again and (circle) the correct options.
5.01

1 Daisy doesn't like (cleaning the kitchen) / *tidying her room*.
2 Milo does the *washing* / *washing-up* at the weekend.
3 His parents *pay* / *thank* him for helping out with the chores.
4 The children's father does *all* / *some* of the cleaning.
5 Their mother *likes* / *doesn't like* cooking.
6 Milo and Daisy do *the washing-up* / *their homework* after dinner.

5 ⭐⭐⭐ Answer the questions.

1 What do you do to help out at home?

_____

2 Who cooks in your family?

_____

3 What chores do you like or hate doing? Why?

_____

LANGUAGE IN ACTION
have to/don't have to

1 ⭐ (Circle) the correct options.

1 I really (*have to*) / *don't have to* tidy my room because I can't find anything.

2 Pat *has to* / *doesn't have to* cycle to school because it's too far for her to walk there.

3 Most children *have to* / *don't have to* go to school on Sundays.

4 You *have to* / *don't have to* wash those jeans. They're clean.

5 There's no bread, so you *have to* / *don't have to* buy more.

2 ⭐⭐ Complete the sentences with the correct form of *have to* and the verb in brackets.

1 Jake ____has to run____ (run) when he's late for school.

2 You _____ (make) your bed because I haven't got time.

3 We _____ (shop) for food because Dad does that.

4 My three-year-old sister _____ (do) anything to help in the house. She's too young.

5 I _____ (wash) the car because we haven't got one.

6 Bill _____ (help) his parents when they're too busy to do everything.

3 ⭐⭐ Put the words in the correct order to make questions.

1 shop / day / dad / Does / to / have / every / your / ?
Does your dad have to shop every day?

2 help / house / have / Do / in / you / to / the / ?
_____

3 the / have / sleep / outside / Does / dog / to / ?
_____

4 carpet / vacuum / have / Do / to / bedroom / you / your / ?
_____

5 children / bed / to / have / be / in / by / Do / nine / the / ?
_____

6 Owen / Does / to / have / leave / breakfast / before / ?
_____

4 ⭐⭐ Look at the table and complete the sentences with the correct form of *have to*.

	Berat	Elif	Ali
do the washing-up	✗	✓	✗
load the washing machine	✗	✓	✗
wash the kitchen floor	✗	✗	✗
tidy up the kitchen	✓	✗	✗
make breakfast	✓	✗	✗
make our beds	✓	✓	✓

1 Elif ___has to do___ the washing-up and load the washing machine.

2 Berat, Elif and Ali _____ the kitchen floor.

3 Ali's very little so he _____ much.

4 Ali only _____ his bed.

5 Berat _____ the kitchen, but he _____ the washing-up.

6 Berat _____ breakfast.

5 ⭐⭐⭐ Complete the text with the correct form of *have to* and the verbs in the box.

carry   do   put   take
tidy up   wash   ~~work~~

My younger sister, Jenny, [1] *doesn't have to work* very hard at school because she's still little, but she and her classmates [2] _____ the classroom at the end of the day so it's nice and clean. They [3] _____ their chairs on top of their desks, but they [4] _____ the floor – the school cleaner, Mr Branston, [5] _____ that. Jenny's got some heavy books, but she [6] _____ them home every day – she can keep them on her shelf in the classroom. When there's homework, Jenny brings the book that she needs home, but she [7] _____ it back to school the next day. I think she's a very good student – just like me!

WRITING

A description of a holiday home

1 ⭐ **Look at the photos and read the description. Which house does it describe: a or b?** _____

> **1** This holiday home is in a quiet place with great views, but it's ¹(also)/ too near enough to a big town. You can drive to the shops and there's a bus ²as well as / too.
>
> **2** The house is a long modern building with four huge bedrooms upstairs. The living room has got big windows, but the windows upstairs are big ³as well / as well as. There's a beautiful tropical garden and there are plants on the balcony ⁴as well as / too.
>
> **3** The very special thing about this house is the home cinema. It's not as big as a real cinema, but you don't have to leave the house! It's really cool because ⁵as well as / also seats for ten people, there's a fridge and a cupboard for yummy snacks! It's the best holiday home in the world!
>
> _Daniel Bell (13), Liverpool_

2 ⭐ (Circle) the correct options (1–5) in the description.

3 ⭐⭐ Read the description again. Are the sentences _T_ (true) or _F_ (false)?

  1 The house is in the centre of a big town.   F

  2 There's no public transport near the house.   ___

  3 There are big windows upstairs.   ___

  4 The house is special because there's a cinema in it.   ___

4 ⭐ Match headings a–c with paragraphs 1–3.

  a What has the house got? ☐

  b What is really special about the house? ☐

  c Where is the house? ☐

Write a description of a holiday home.

PLAN

5 ⭐⭐ **Find a photo of a holiday home online or in a magazine. Make notes.**

  1 Where is your holiday home?

    _____

    Why do you like it?

    _____

  2 What rooms, furniture and other things has it got?

    _____

  3 Why is your holiday home special?

    _____

WRITE

6 ⭐⭐⭐ **Write your description. Remember to include adjectives with (_not_) _as … as_, (_not_) _enough_ and _have to/don't have to_.**

CHECK

7 **Do you …**

  • use the phrases from the _Useful language_ box (see Student's Book, p65)?

  • have three paragraphs?

  • explain why your holiday home is special?

VOCABULARY

1 (Circle) the correct options.

1 Ellie is sitting in a comfortable *carpet / armchair* and reading a comic.

2 Take the cups out of the dishwasher and put them in the *cupboard / fridge*.

3 After he irons his shirts, Tom puts them carefully in his *desk / wardrobe*.

4 We need some more *shelves / carpets* above the sink in the bathroom.

5 Don't forget to clean the *floor / sink* after you brush your teeth.

6 There's milk all over the kitchen *ceiling / floor*. Did someone break a cup?

7 Mum has a special place in her *desk / chest of drawers* for scarves and gloves.

8 Berto was vacuuming the living room *shelves / carpet* when he found his lost key.

9 There's bread on the table and butter and cheese in the *fridge / sink*.

10 Ryan's got a nice *desk / bookcase* in his room, but he never does his homework there.

2 Complete the household chores in the spidergram.

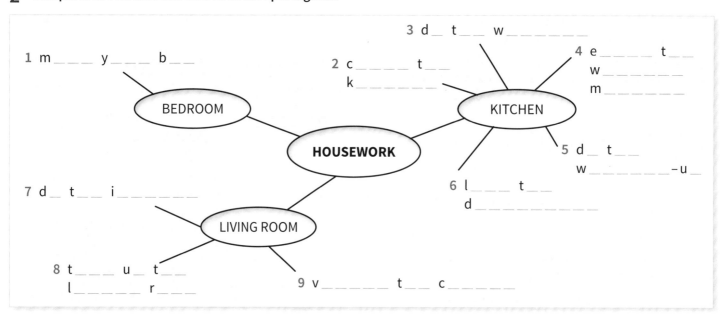

3 d _ t ___ w _____

1 m ____ y ____ b ___

2 c _____ t __
k _____

4 e _____ t ___
w _____
m _____

BEDROOM

KITCHEN

HOUSEWORK

5 d _ t ___
w _____ -u _ _

7 d _ t ___ i _____

6 l ____ t ___
d _____

LIVING ROOM

8 t ____ u _ t ___
l _____ r ____

9 v _____ t ___ c _____

LANGUAGE IN ACTION

3 Rewrite the sentences with (*not*) *as ... as* or (*not*) *enough* and the adjectives in brackets.

1 Your house is the same size as my house. (big)

Your house _____ *is as big as my house* _____ .

2 The weather is warmer today. (cold)

The weather today _____

3 Sam is more nervous than Jack. (relaxed)

Sam _____ .

4 Nicky is too young to watch that film. (old)

Nicky _____ .

5 I don't need a bigger desk than this one. (big)

This desk _____ .

6 Frank is stronger than his brother. (strong)

Frank's brother _____ .

7 Is there enough sugar in your coffee? (sweet)

Is your coffee _____ ?

8 Sofia and her mother are 1.62 metres tall. (tall)

Sofia _____ .

4 Complete the sentences with the correct form of *have to*.

1 We _____ do all the washing-up. We've got a dishwasher.

2 You _____ put the cups on the top shelf, not on the bottom.

3 Maisie _____ help in the garden. Her dad does that.

4 We _____ wash our clothes by hand. We use the washing machine.

5 You _____ give me a knife and fork. I can use chopsticks.

6 Mr Kelly _____ clean the school windows. That's his job.

7 You _____ help me, thanks. I know what to do.

8 They _____ buy a new vacuum cleaner. Their old one broke.

CUMULATIVE LANGUAGE

5 Complete the conversation with the missing words. (Circle) the correct options.

DAD   Hey, Kevin, come over here. I ¹_____ at some holiday websites.

KEVIN   Oh, great. Can I take the tent you ²_____ me for my birthday?

DAD   Well, your mum ³_____ camping.

KEVIN   Oh, but Dad, tents are ⁴_____ these days than they were in the past.

DAD   Yes, but I ⁵_____ about a holiday home, you know, with a pool.

KEVIN   A holiday home isn't ⁶_____ a campsite, Dad.

DAD   ⁷_____ where we stayed last summer?

KEVIN   Yeah, it was nice, but it wasn't ⁸_____ for me.

DAD   A holiday home is definitely ⁹_____.

KEVIN   Yeah, but it's boring. There aren't ¹⁰_____ other kids to hang out with.

DAD   Well, I'm sorry your mother and I aren't ¹¹_____ for you, Kevin.

KEVIN   No, Dad, I didn't mean that. But you ¹²_____ agree: you're not as much fun as my friends!

1	a look	b	'm looking	c	do look
2	a buy	b	buyed	c	bought
3	a not like	b	doesn't like	c	don't like
4	a better	b	good	c	best
5	a were thinking	b	was thinking	c	did thought
6	a as interesting as	b	more interesting as	c	interesting than
7	a Are you liking	b	Were you liking	c	Did you like
8	a enough exciting	b	very exciting enough	c	exciting enough
9	a most comfortable as	b	more comfortable	c	the more comfortable
10	a some	b	one	c	any
11	a cooler enough	b	enough cool	c	cool enough
12	a has to	b	don't have to	c	have to

6 HIDDEN DANGER

VOCABULARY
Accidents and injuries

1 ⭐ **Put the letters in the correct order to make words and phrases about accidents and injuries.**

1 eb ttneib ___be bitten___
2 tih _____
3 usbrie _____
4 npsira _____
5 uct _____
6 eb gutsn _____

7 runb _____
8 lafl fof _____
9 psil _____
10 tarccsh _____
11 kebra _____
12 ptir vroe _____

2 ⭐ (Circle) **the odd one out.**

1 break / bruise /(slip) **your arm**
2 fall off / sprain / trip over **a bike**
3 be cut / be stung / be bitten **by an insect**
4 scratch / cut / burn **your finger with a knife**
5 hit / break / bruise **your head on the door**

3 ⭐ **Match 1–6 with a–f.**

1 Jeremy was stung ⬚e⬚
2 The bruise on my arm ⬚⬚
3 You can't play football ⬚⬚
4 I didn't see my bag ⬚⬚
5 They were running round the pool ⬚⬚
6 He fell off his surfboard ⬚⬚

a and I tripped over it.
b if you break your leg.
c when they slipped on the wet floor.
d and into the sea.
e on his leg by a bee.
f is now black and blue.

4 ⭐⭐ **Complete the sentences with the correct form of words and phrases from Exercise 1.**

1 Henry __sprained__ his ankle running for the bus.
2 The cat _____ my arm when I picked it up.
3 You can easily _____ your hand on a campfire.
4 You can _____ by mosquitoes when you camp near water.
5 My grandma _____ her finger on a sharp knife.
6 He _____ his head as he was getting out of the car.

5 ⭐⭐ **Complete the chat with the correct form of the words and phrases in the box.**

> bruise   ~~fall off~~   hit   not break
> sprain   trip over

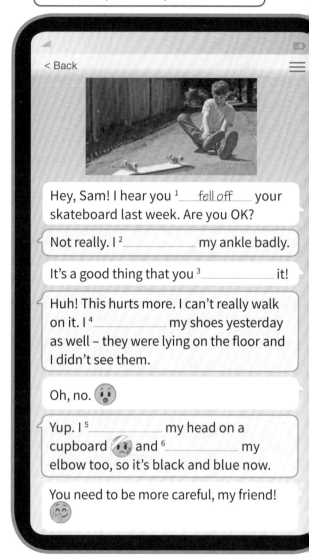

< Back

Hey, Sam! I hear you ¹__fell off__ your skateboard last week. Are you OK?

Not really. I ²_____ my ankle badly.

It's a good thing that you ³_____ it!

Huh! This hurts more. I can't really walk on it. I ⁴_____ my shoes yesterday as well – they were lying on the floor and I didn't see them.

Oh, no. 😲

Yup. I ⁵_____ my head on a cupboard 🤕 and ⁶_____ my elbow too, so it's black and blue now.

You need to be more careful, my friend! 🤔

Explore it! 🖱

Guess the correct answer.

Both male and female / Only male / Only female mosquitoes bite humans.

Find another interesting fact about mosquitoes. Then send a question in an email to a classmate or ask them it in the next class.

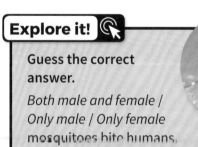

READING

An online article

1 ⭐ Read the article and write the headings in the correct places (1–4).

> Burns   Do not eat or drink!   Falls   Things up noses

● ● ●

DANGER AT HOME!

HOME | STORIES | PHOTOS

1 _____

You probably think that the most dangerous room in the house is the kitchen, but in fact most accidents happen in the living room! Small children can get serious burns from hot drinks or open fires. Candles are also the cause of many accidents in the living room – a candle near a curtain can start a horrible house fire!

2 _____

Many people go to hospital after getting poisoned, especially young children. Do you sometimes paint your bedroom? When you finish painting a wall, put the paints in a safe place so that young children don't try to drink them. Medicines, too, should be in a top bathroom cupboard – they shouldn't be easy for kids to get.

3 _____

This is a surprising, but common, accident. Young children often put the strangest things up their noses: frozen peas, crayons, chips … . They think it's funny, but it can be serious. These things get stuck and it sometimes needs a hospital visit to get them out.

4 _____

Falling is the most common accident in the home. Be careful: climbing up a ladder to get something down from a high shelf can be very risky. This happens most often to people over 65 and kids under 15. And remember: young children mustn't play near open windows – 4,000 children fall out of them every year in the UK, so watch out.

2 ⭐⭐ Read the article again and check the meaning of these words in a dictionary. Then complete the sentences.

> candles   ladder   ~~medicine~~
> poison   risky   stuck

1 Judy was ill last year and she's still taking a lot of ___medicine___ .

2 My little brother had seven _____ on his birthday cake.

3 Drinking dirty or polluted water can _____ you.

4 It's very _____ to light a candle and leave it near a small child.

5 We needed a _____ to get the boxes down from the top shelf.

6 My hand got _____ under the sofa and I couldn't get it out.

3 ⭐⭐ Read the article again. Answer the questions.

1 Which room is the most dangerous, according to the article?
the living room

2 How can house fires start in the living room?
_____

3 What's the best place to keep medicines?
_____

4 Why do little children put things up their noses?
_____

5 Which age groups have the most accidents with falls?
_____

6 How can an open window be dangerous?
_____

4 ⭐⭐⭐ Answer the questions with your own ideas.

1 Which fact in the article surprised you the most? Why?
_____

2 Do you light fires or candles at home? When?
_____

LANGUAGE IN ACTION
should/shouldn't and *must/mustn't*

1 ⭐ **Complete the sentences with *should* or *shouldn't*.**

1 You ___should___ always be careful with candles.

2 You _____ leave a lighted candle in an empty room.

3 Dad says that we _____ tidy up our shoes.

4 Maybe we _____ have a smoke alarm in the classroom.

5 You _____ take other people's medicine.

6 We _____ prevent as many accidents as we can.

2 ⭐ **Complete the sentences with the words in the box.**

> should be   should do   should send
> shouldn't drink   shouldn't laugh   ~~shouldn't swim~~

1 There's a red flag on the beach, so you _shouldn't swim_ here.

2 My uncle had an accident at work. I _____ him a card.

3 It's very icy today, so you _____ careful that you don't slip.

4 Oliver was stung by a bee. You _____ at him – it's not funny!

5 My brother's got a broken arm, so I _____ the washing-up.

6 Hey, you _____ that medicine! It's not fruit juice!

3 ⭐⭐ **Complete the poster with *should* or *shouldn't* and a suitable verb.**

Can't sleep at bedtime?
Can't get up in the morning?

Here's some advice from SLEEP NURSE!

You ¹ _should do_ exercise in the fresh air every day.

You ² _____ tea or coffee in the evening.

You ³ _____ to quiet relaxing music.

You ⁴ _____ scary movies in bed.

You ⁵ _____ your phone in a different room.

You ⁶ _____ off your light before you go to sleep.

4 ⭐⭐ **Complete the sentences about the signs using *must* or *mustn't*. Sometimes there is more than one possible answer.**

1 You _mustn't park here_ .

2 You _____ .

3 You _____ .

4 You _____ .

5 You _____ .

6 You _____ .

5 ⭐⭐ **Circle the best options to complete the conversation.**

PAULA I think you ¹*should* / *shouldn't* / *must* come to judo club, Lola. It's really good!

LOLA Do you really think I ²*should* / *must* / *mustn't*? I'm not very sporty.

PAULA I know, but Mum says we ³*should* / *shouldn't* / *must* do at least one after-school activity, so you have to choose one.

LOLA OK, what are the rules? What do I need to know?

PAULA First, you ⁴*shouldn't* / *must* / *mustn't* be late because you can't come in once the class starts. Second, you ⁵*should* / *must* / *mustn't* bring judo clothes – you can't wear normal clothes. And the most important thing: you ⁶*should* / *must* / *mustn't* listen to everything the instructor says. Judo can be dangerous.

LOLA Mmm, it sounds a bit scary!

VOCABULARY AND LISTENING

Parts of the body

A radio interview

1 ⭐ **Find 11 more words for parts of the body in the word search. The words can be in any direction.**

A	K	E	E	H	C	C	L	V
R	W	D	O	C	H	I	N	N
F	O	R	E	H	E	A	D	M
Y	B	K	J	T	S	F	K	E
U	L	C	P	E	T	M	N	C
L	E	E	H	E	X	Z	E	I
A	C	N	S	T	T	O	E	A
W	R	I	S	T	V	N	W	N
R	E	D	L	U	O	H	S	R

2 ⭐ (Circle) **the correct options.**

1 Marie's hair grew over her (forehead)/ *neck*, almost to her eyes.

2 The boys' *chins* / *cheeks* were red when they came in from the cold.

3 Joe walked on broken glass and cut his *wrist* / *heel*.

4 Our teacher wore a lovely long scarf round her *neck* / *elbow*.

5 Olympic swimmers often have very wide *chests* / *elbows*.

6 The girl fell off her bike and hurt her *teeth* / *knee*.

7 Ballet dancers wear special shoes so they can dance on their *toes* / *elbows*.

8 She was wearing three thin gold bracelets round her *shoulder* / *wrist*.

🎧 **3** ⭐ **Look at the pictures about a story. What do you think happened? Listen and put the pictures in the correct order (1–6).**
6.01

a

b

c

d
1

e

f

🎧 **4** ⭐⭐ **Listen again. Are the sentences *T* (true) or *F* (false)?**
6.01

1 Toby was on the boat with a friend. ___F___

2 Toby says dolphins can sometimes be dangerous. _____

3 The boys didn't know what the dolphins were doing. _____

4 The shark disappeared after about an hour. _____

5 One dolphin injured Toby's shoulder. _____

6 People can find more animal stories on the radio station's website. _____

5 ⭐⭐⭐ **Answer the questions with your own ideas.**

1 Which other animals are especially clever?

_____

2 Which other animals sometimes protect humans? How?

_____

LANGUAGE IN ACTION
Zero conditional and first conditional

1 ⭐ Complete the zero conditional sentences with the correct form of the verbs in brackets.

1 People _don't swim_ (not swim) here when they ___see___ (see) the red flag on the beach.

2 When sharks _____ (get) hungry, they _____ (be) a danger to swimmers.

3 Broken glass _____ (cut) your toes if you _____ (not wear) shoes.

4 Swimmers _____ (get) very cold if they _____ (stay) in the sea too long.

5 If the temperature _____ (fall) below 0 °C, water _____ (turn) into ice.

6 If a bee _____ (sting) you, it really _____ (hurt).

2 ⭐⭐ Write zero conditional sentences.

1 if / I / drink coffee at night / I / not sleep
If I drink coffee at night, I don't sleep.

2 if / we / study hard / we / do well in our tests
_____

3 when / Helena / feel ill / she / not come to school
_____

4 my little brother / fall over / if / he / run too fast
_____

5 I / feel really bad / when / I / forget my friend's birthday
_____

6 if / you / ring the doctor after nine / nobody / answer
_____

3 ⭐⭐ Complete the zero conditional sentences with the correct form of the verbs in the box.

| break die eat fall get go ~~look~~ not rain ~~swim~~ walk |

1 Ross always ___swims___ in the river if it ___looks___ safe.

2 Children _____ bad teeth if they _____ too much sugar.

3 If it _____ all summer, some plants and animals _____ .

4 Older people _____ over easily when they _____ on ice.

5 You _____ to hospital if you _____ your leg.

4 ⭐⭐ (Circle) the correct options.

1 If you (see) / will see a crocodile, you'll be in trouble.

2 I'll carry your bags if your shoulders *will hurt* / *hurt*.

3 If your cat scratches Laura, she *isn't* / *won't be* happy.

4 The roads will be dangerous if it *snows* / *will snow* tonight.

5 There will be an accident if they *aren't* / *won't be* more careful.

6 If she *will run* / *runs* too fast, her chest will start to hurt.

5 ⭐⭐ Complete the first conditional sentences in the text with the correct form of the verbs in brackets.

Don't get lost!

If you [1] ___walk___ (walk) a lot in the countryside, it's possible that one day you [2] _____ (get) lost. If this happens, sit down and eat and drink something. If you [3] _____ (feel) calm, you [4] _____ (think) more clearly. Can you send a text or make a call? If you [5] _____ (make) contact with someone, [6] _____ you (know) how to direct them to where you are? If you [7] _____ (look) around, you [8] _____ probably _____ (recognise) something. Remember to always take the correct equipment so you don't get lost in the first place. You [9] _____ (be) better prepared if you [10] _____ (pack) a map and a compass before you go!

WRITING
A blog post

1 **Read the blog post. Do you agree with the advice?** _____

● ● ●

The Climbers' Climbing Blog

Thanks for reading my blog! Here are a few of my readers' questions and my answers.

I always bruise my knees and elbows when I'm rock climbing. What should I do to avoid that? **Spidergirl**

You should buy some knee and elbow pads. But [1] *make sure / that's why* that you climb in the correct way. You won't bruise anything if you're careful. [2] *If you ask me, / Make sure* you need some expert advice and maybe a lesson or two!

I'm 11 and I'd love to go climbing with my older brothers, but they say I'm too young. What's a good age to start climbing? **Katya**

If you're tall and strong enough, you'll be able to climb now! [3] *That's why / I'd say* it's safe to start climbing at your age if you start with small climbs and you have good climbers with you. If you're careful, you'll be fine. Enjoy!

When's the safest time to go climbing? I only climb in the summer, but I want to do more. **Barbara**

In the UK, spring and summer are the best times. You'll slip and fall if you climb on wet rocks. [4] *Make sure / That's why* you shouldn't do it on rainy days. And of course, you must never climb in snowy or icy weather if you don't have special equipment.

That's all for now. Have fun, and happy climbing!

2 **Circle the correct options (1–4) in the blog post.**

3 ⭐⭐ **Read the blog post again. Write S (Spidergirl), K (Katya) or B (Barbara) for each sentence.**

1 She wants to know the best time for climbing. ___
2 The blogger thinks she should have classes. ___
3 The blogger says she should go with other climbers. ___

4 ⭐⭐ **Read the blog post again and circle the correct answers.**

1 Rock climbers should wear knee and elbow pads to avoid … .
   a bruises **b** falls **c** climbing incorrectly

2 Katya's brothers think she's not … enough to start climbing.
   a tall **b** old **c** strong

3 Katya should start with … climbs.
   a good **b** short **c** careful

4 Barbara doesn't climb on … days.
   a sunny **b** summer **c** winter

5 Climbers need special equipment in … weather.
   a summer **b** rainy **c** icy

Write a blog post to give safety advice.

PLAN

5 ⭐⭐ **Choose an activity that you do. Think of three questions about doing it safely. Make notes for the answers.**

1 _____
2 _____
3 _____

WRITE

6 ⭐⭐⭐ **Write your blog post. Remember to include an introduction, three questions and answers, an ending and phrases from the *Useful language* box (see Student's Book, p77).**

CHECK

7 Do you …
- answer each question?
- use *should/shouldn't* and *must/mustn't*?
- use vocabulary from this unit?

VOCABULARY

1 Complete the crossword. Use the clues.

Across

2 You … on icy roads.

7 A … round your eye is called a 'black eye'.

9 You … … objects on the floor if you don't see them.

10 Don't … your hand on the fire!

12 She … her head on the cupboard door.

Down

1 It hurts a lot when you … your ankle.

3 Don't stand on the wall or you'll … … !

4 Rugby players often … their noses.

5 You can … … by a bee if you make it angry.

6 You can … … by mosquitoes if you leave the window open.

8 Does your cat sometimes … you?

11 He … his foot on a sharp rock.

2 Complete the words for parts of the body with the missing vowels.

1 f _ r _ h _ _ d

2 h _ _ l

3 _ l b _ w

4 k n _ _

5 ch _ n

6 n _ c k

7 ch _ s t

8 sh _ _ l d _ r

9 ch _ _ k

10 t _ _ t h

11 w r _ s t

12 t _ _

LANGUAGE IN ACTION

3 Are the <u>underlined</u> words correct in the sentences? Correct the incorrect ones.

1 You <u>mustn't</u> drive on the left on British roads.
____must____

2 If she likes helping sick people, she <u>should</u> become a nurse. _____

3 You <u>mustn't</u> put metal in a microwave. _____

4 Cyclists <u>mustn't</u> stop when they see a stop sign. _____

5 Children <u>should</u> brush their teeth after eating sweets. _____

6 You <u>mustn't</u> buy a ticket when you travel on public transport. _____

7 You <u>should</u> go rock climbing in the rain. It's incredibly dangerous! _____

4 Put the words in the correct order to make conditional sentences. Add commas where necessary.

1 you are bitten / it hurts / If / by a mosquito
_____

2 warm clothes / we wear / We won't get cold / if
_____

3 If / I won't / I see a red flag / go swimming
_____

4 be happy / you wake him up / if / Nikita won't
_____

5 When / football indoors / it rains / we usually play
_____

6 you go cycling / to wear a helmet / when / It is sensible
_____

5 Complete the conversation with the missing words. (Circle) the correct options.

MARINA Do we ¹_____ go this way, Diego? Are you sure it's right?

DIEGO Yes, I'm sure. The map says if we ²_____ the path, we get to the hostel.

MARINA Did you check the route before we ³_____?

DIEGO Of course! But we ⁴_____ hurry. It's getting dark. Come on!

MARINA If I try to run, I ⁵_____ over. Ouch! Hey, Diego! Come back! Oh, no. My ankle!

DIEGO What's the problem? Why ⁶_____ there?

MARINA I ⁷_____ after you ⁸_____ I fell and sprained my ankle. It hurts!

DIEGO Oh, no! You should be more careful! Does it feel better if you ⁹_____ still? Or do you think you can walk on it?

MARINA Not sure. Is the hostel far from here?

DIEGO Well, I don't really know. Is your ankle still ¹⁰_____ it was?

MARINA Yes, it is. We could phone for help. Does the phone work up here?

DIEGO No, sorry. Listen, you stay here and I'll go for help. I ¹¹_____ long if I run. But you ¹²_____ move.

MARINA Don't worry, I can't! And please, be quick!

1	a	must	b	should	c	have to
2	a	follow	b	will follow	c	followed
3	a	leave	b	left	c	were leaving
4	a	mustn't	b	shouldn't	c	should
5	a	won't fall	b	'll fall	c	fell
6	a	do you sit	b	will you sit	c	are you sitting
7	a	ran	b	was running	c	'm running
8	a	when	b	as	c	while
9	a	sat	b	sit	c	will sit
10	a	as worse as	b	worst	c	as bad as
11	a	won't be	b	be	c	'm not
12	a	must	b	should	c	mustn't

GET CONNECTED

VOCABULARY
Communication and technology

1 ⭐ **Find ten more communication and technology words and phrases in the word snake.**

messageuploaddownloadappchipssocialmediadevicevideochatemojiscreenssoftware

2 ⭐ ⊂Circle⊃ **the correct options.**

1 I usually send my mother a *device* /(*message*) if I'm not home on time.

2 When his dad's working in the US, Thomas often does a *video chat* / *social media* with him.

3 You can listen to music on your tablet or any other mobile *emoji* / *device*.

4 Our IT teacher wrote some *chips* / *software* for checking homework.

5 Blogs and other types of *social media* / *video chat* are great fun.

6 Iris dropped her phone and broke the *app* /*screen* on it.

3 ⭐⭐ **Match the definitions with words from Exercise 1.**

1 copy information to a computer system or to the Internet ___upload___

2 copy information onto a phone, tablet, laptop, etc. from the Internet or a computer _____

3 the short word for an 'application', for example, Spotify or Facebook _____

4 a digital picture that shows a feeling or emotion

_____

5 a flat surface on a TV or computer where you can see words or pictures _____

6 it's very small: the 'brain' inside a computer or phone _____

4 ⭐ **Match the words to make different collocations. Sometimes there is more than one possible answer.**

computer
~~download~~ social
electronic send
upload

media
devices
a message
screen ~~software~~
photos

*download software,*_____

_____

_____

5 ⭐⭐ **Complete the phone instructions with the correct form of words and phrases from Exercise 1.**

Thank you for buying a Techtime phone. When you turn on your new ¹ ___device___ for the first time, you will see an icon for 'Games Shop' at the bottom left of the ² _____ . Here, you can ³_____ all your favourite social media, music and news

⁴ _____ , like WhatsApp and Spotify. To write a ⁵_____ using text or email, press on one of your contacts in the contacts list. The Techtime 1000 has also got an excellent camera, so ⁶_____ with friends and family is easy!

Explore it! 🖱

True or false?

The average person checks their phone ten times a day.

Find another interesting fact about phones. Then send a question in an email to a classmate or ask them it in the next class.

READING
A magazine article

1 ⭐ Look at the photo and the title of the article. What do you think the article is about? Read the article and check your ideas. _____

High-tech or no-tech?

Juan Carlos García investigates how a school in California's Silicon Valley uses technology – or doesn't!

Silicon Valley in California has become the world centre of technology, innovation and social media. It's home to some of the world's biggest tech companies. So, with all this technology around, you probably think that all schools in Silicon Valley use lots of computers, laptops and tablets in their classrooms, right? Wrong! In Masters Secondary School, the school I visited, there isn't a tablet, screen or laptop anywhere. The classrooms have plants, traditional wooden desks and even blackboards with coloured chalks!

So why don't they use technology? The surprising thing is that the parents of these children – many of them technology experts at major tech companies – believe that bringing technology to class isn't a good idea! Many think that it doesn't help young people use their own minds. So, in this school, there are no electronic teaching devices in the classroom. Teachers here think that kids use their imagination better without them!

This means that students don't use the Internet to study or download apps to help them learn, and they use pens and paper to write, not tablets or laptops. They study their main subjects through artistic activities like music and painting. One student told me, 'Our teachers believe that technology will only be helpful when we're older and we know how and when to use it properly.'

So even the tech experts think that technology has its limits! High-tech or no-tech: which is the best? What do you think?

2 ⭐⭐ Read the article again and check the meaning of these words in a dictionary. Then complete the sentences.

> expert ~~imagination~~ innovation major minds properly

1 I'm not very good at writing stories because I've got no _imagination_ .

2 My aunt knows a lot about computers. She's a technology _____ .

3 When you use this dictionary app _____ , it's very easy to find the words you want.

4 This young company is famous for its _____ and new ideas.

5 My brother made a _____ decision to move to the US to study.

6 People who develop software have got creative _____ .

3 ⭐⭐ Read the article again. Are the sentences *T* (true) or *F* (false)?

1 Juan Carlos visited the school to learn about new classroom technology. _F_

2 The school is home to technology and innovation. ___

3 Juan Carlos expected to find a lot of electronic teaching devices in the school. ___

4 Some parents think that classroom technology stops young people from thinking creatively. ___

5 Students learn through artistic subjects. ___

6 Teachers believe that technology will never help students learn. ___

4 ⭐⭐⭐ Answer the questions with your own ideas.

1 How do some schools use technology in class?

_____

2 What electronic devices do you use in class to help you learn?

_____

LANGUAGE IN ACTION

Present perfect: affirmative and negative

1 ⭐ **Complete the table with the correct past participles.**

be	was	¹ ___been___
change	changed	² _____
choose	chose	³ _____
do	did	⁴ _____
hear	heard	⁵ _____
learn	learned	⁶ _____
design	designed	⁷ _____
see	saw	⁸ _____

2 ⭐⭐ **Complete the sentences with the present perfect form of the verbs in Exercise 1.**

1 Maisie _has learned_ to use her new phone now.

2 Technology _____ the way we learn.

3 The reporter _____ to many different schools in the US.

4 I _____ the new *Mission Impossible* film: don't miss it, it's great.

5 The students _____ their subjects for next year.

6 We _____ our maths and ICT homework.

7 I _____ a website for our basketball team.

8 Paul _____ the news, so you don't have to tell him.

3 ⭐ **Make the sentences negative.**

1 I've charged my phone.

I haven't charged my phone.

2 Sergey's forgotten his password.

_____

3 Wanda's broken her watch.

_____

4 We've bought a new computer.

_____

5 They've turned on the TV.

_____

6 I've asked for more information.

_____

4 ⭐ **Write sentences with the present perfect.**

1 I / not finish / my homework for tomorrow

I haven't finished my homework for tomorrow.

2 Gerrie / not read / anything about Silicon Valley

_____

3 we / look for / some better information

_____

4 they / buy / a new computer online

_____

5 he / use / the latest software

_____

6 the boys / not ring / their parents

_____

5 ⭐⭐ **Choose the correct verb in each pair. Then complete the text with the present perfect form.**

Hi Jess,

Good news! I ¹ _'ve thrown_ (throw / push) away my old tablet! Mum and Dad ² _____ (sell / buy) me a new laptop. I ³ _____ (upload / download) some great music software from the Internet and I ⁴ _____ (decide / forget) to make a website for my band. I'm not sure if I told you, but I ⁵ _____ (stop / start) a band. Nico and I ⁶ _____ (write / listen) some music together. Nico ⁷ _____ (give / choose) the songs that we want to sing, but we still ⁸ _____ (not film / not record) anything.

More soon!

Theo

VOCABULARY AND LISTENING
Getting around

1 ⭐ Complete the transport phrases with the missing vowels.

1 g o _o_ _o_ n f _o_ _o_ t
2 g _ t _ n _ tr _ _ n
3 g _ t _ ff _ b _ s
4 g _ t _ _ t _ f _ c _ r
5 g _ t _ nt _ _ t _ x _
6 g _ by tr _ m
7 t _ k _ _ pl _ n _

2 ⭐ Match 1–6 with a–d.

1 Our visitors got into [d]
2 We planned to catch [ ]
3 I usually go by [ ]
4 If you miss your bus, [ ]
5 Which tram stop should I [ ]
6 Is it better to cycle or go [ ]

a bike when it isn't raining.
b you can catch the next one.
c on foot?
d their car and drove away.
e a plane from Manchester Airport.
f get off at?

3 ⭐ Circle the correct options.

1 I *get* / *go* by tram when I visit my friends in town.
2 Pete always goes to school *on* / *by* bike.
3 I get off the bus at this stop and go *by* / *on* foot from here.
4 My friend's *taken* / *got into* a plane to Sardinia.
5 Get *on* / *off* the train and find a seat by the window.
6 If you go *on* / *by* the underground, you get there quicker.
7 They can *catch* / *go by* a bus outside their house.
8 Marie got out *off* / *of* the car and hit her head on the door.

A radio interview

🎧 4 ⭐ Listen to the interview. Do Ellie and Joe think space tourism is just science fiction?
7.01

_____

🎧 5 ⭐⭐ Listen again and circle the correct answers.
7.01

1 The interview takes place … .
  a in a radio studio   b at a school
  (c) at a technology fair

2 Joe says he … to drive.
  a loves   b doesn't need
  c hasn't learned

3 Ellie likes the idea of … .
  a driverless cars   b more bikes
  c faster bikes

4 She's seen an exhibit about … in space.
  a films   b astronauts   c travel

5 Joe thinks rockets to space will be … today's jet planes.
  a the same as b different from c similar to

6 In Ellie's opinion, tourist trips to Mars in the next 20 years are … .
  a possible   b impossible   c a problem

6 ⭐⭐⭐ Answer the questions.

1 In your opinion, is a holiday on Mars just science fiction? Why / Why not?

_____

_____

2 If it becomes possible to go on holiday in space, do you think you will go? Why / Why not?

_____

_____

LANGUAGE IN ACTION
will/won't, may and *might*

1 ⭐ **Complete the sentences with *will* or *won't*.**

1 The photos you post online _____will_____ stay there for a long time.

2 Workers worry that robots _____ replace them and take their jobs.

3 I _____ work in another country in the future – I hate travelling.

4 Cars _____ need drivers in the future because of new driverless technology.

5 I think cities _____ become more bike-friendly in future years because of all the traffic.

2 ⭐ (Circle) **the correct options.**

1 Maybe you should take a coat. It *will* / (*might*) be cold.

2 Phones will always be expensive. They *won't* / *might* get cheaper.

3 It's not certain, but we *will* / *may* go to school by helicopter in the future.

4 They *will* / *may* go by train, but they still haven't decided.

5 He *will* / *might* have his own bike one day – he's sure of that!

3 ⭐⭐ (Circle) **the correct options below to complete the email.**

● ● ●

TO: Josh	FROM: Lindy

Hi Josh,

I'm on a train with my mum and dad. They ¹_____ be away for the weekend, so I'm staying with my uncle Ted. It ²_____ be much fun there – it never is, 😟 but I'm sure I ³_____ chat to friends online. But then, who knows – there ⁴_____ be wi-fi in his house – I haven't asked! 😮 I'm sure he ⁵_____ have a TV, though – everyone's got one! I ⁶_____ speak to you online this afternoon, but I don't know yet. Uncle Ted wants to go birdwatching! 😫
Lindy

1	(a) will	b won't	c might
2	a may not	b will	c won't
3	a may	b might	c will
4	a might not	b won't	c may
5	a won't	b will	c may
6	a may not	b will	c may

Infinitive of purpose

4 ⭐⭐ **Rewrite the sentences with the infinitive of purpose.**

1 My sister Maddie and I went to Crich. We wanted to visit the Tramway Museum.

My sister Maddie and I went to Crich to visit the Tramway Museum.

2 First Maddie went online. She checked the train times.

_____

_____

3 We walked to the station. We bought the tickets there.

_____

_____

4 I left the house at 6 am. I wanted to catch the first train.

_____

_____

5 Maddie wanted to stop at a shop. She needed to buy some sandwiches.

_____

_____

6 We got on the train quickly. That's how we got the best seats.

_____

_____

5 ⭐⭐ **Complete the text with the verbs and phrases in the box.**

> may buy   might fly   to drive   ~~to get~~
> to go   will travel

I normally use public transport ¹ _to get_ around. For example, ² _____ to school, I get the bus or I catch a tram. I ³ _____ a motorbike when I'm old enough, or maybe a car. I really don't know how my children ⁴ _____ in the future. Maybe they will have amazing machines ⁵ _____ around in, or they ⁶ _____ through the air. Who knows?

WRITING
An article

1 ⭐ **Read the article. Then** (circle) **the correct answer below.**

Technology has changed the way we ... our friends.

a make contact with   b care for
c have fun with

STAYING IN TOUCH: THEN AND NOW

① The way we communicate with our friends has changed a lot. ¹____ For instance, when our grandparents were young, there were no mobile phones, and what's ²_____, some families didn't even have a telephone at home. To phone a friend, people needed to go to a public phone box.

② In contrast, today there are lots of ways of contacting friends. For ³_____, almost everyone can use a smartphone at any time and in any place. Posting status updates is easy with technology, such ⁴_____ online chats and messaging apps. In ⁵_____, we can send photos and videos to share special moments.

③ Some people think that friends might never meet face-to-face in the future. However, I don't think that will happen. It may become easier to 'see' each other without actually meeting up, but it will always be more fun to sit and chat together.

2 ⭐⭐ **Complete the article with the words in the box.**

| addition   as   example   ~~for~~   more |

3 ⭐ **Read the article again and match 1–5 with a–e.**

1 In the past, there were   ☐ d
2 People needed to use a phone box   ☐
3 Today we can use   ☐
4 It's easier now to share   ☐
5 It will always be more fun   ☐

a photos and videos with friends.
b smartphones to make calls at any time.
c to meet our friends face-to-face.
d no mobile phones.
e to make contact with their friends.

4 ⭐ **Read the article again and write the correct paragraph number (1–3).**

a Which paragraph is about what might happen in the future?

_____

b Which paragraph mentions old technology? _____

c Which paragraph describes ways of communicating today?

_____

Write an article about doing homework.

PLAN

5 ⭐⭐ **Think about homework in the past, present and future. Make notes for your three paragraphs.**
   1 How people did homework in the past:
   _____
   2 Technology for doing homework today:
   _____
   3 Predictions for the future:
   _____

WRITE

6 ⭐⭐⭐ **Write your article. Remember to include past and present tenses, and predictions with *will/won't and may/ might (not).***

CHECK

7 **Do you ...**
   • have three paragraphs?
   • use expressions from the *Useful language* box (see Student's Book, p89)?
   • make certain and uncertain predictions for the future?

VOCABULARY

1 Put the letters in the correct order to make communication and technology words.

1 p a p _____

2 d v o i e t c a h _____

3 j i o m e _____

4 d o u l a p _____

5 l o i s c a d m i a e _____

6 w r o s t e f a _____

7 c r e n e s _____

8 p i h c _____

9 o w o d n l d a _____

10 v i e e d c _____

11 s g a e s e m _____

2 Look at the photos. What are the people doing? Complete the sentences with phrases for getting around.

LANGUAGE IN ACTION

3 Complete the conversation with the present perfect form of the verbs in brackets.

DAD Jon, stop playing computer games now. It's time to eat.

JON I ¹_____ (not play) any games this evening, Dad! And I ²_____ (finish) my homework.

DAD Oh, OK. Well, that's good. I ³_____ (make) your favourite dinner.

JON Great, thanks. I ⁴_____ (send) Mum a message, but she ⁵_____ (not reply).

DAD Well, she ⁶_____ (fly) to Miami, so there's a time difference. I ⁷_____ (check) my emails too, but I ⁸_____ (not hear) from her either. I'm sure she'll call us later.

1 Anna is _____*going on foot*_____.

2 Charlie is _____.

3 Helga is _____.

4 Aki and Ena are _____.

5 David is _____.

6 Maria is _____.

4 Complete the dialogues with the infinitive of purpose or *will/won't*, *may* or *might* (*not*). Use the verbs in the boxes. Sometimes there is more than one possible answer.

have   not have   print

A Can I use your printer ¹_____ these photos, please?

B I'm not sure. I ²_____ enough paper – I need to check. If there isn't enough, I think my dad ³_____ some.

get   not take

A What time do we have to leave ⁴_____ to the cinema by six?

B We have lots of time, and it ⁵_____ long to get there – just five minutes.

be able to   play

A Do I need to download an app ⁶_____ this game?

B Mmm, I don't really know. You ⁷_____ play it without the app. Let's see.

be   edit

A What software does Harry use ⁸_____ his videos?

B I don't know, but he ⁹_____ here in a minute so you can ask him. OK?

CUMULATIVE LANGUAGE

5 Complete the conversation with the missing words. (Circle) the correct options.

CLARE Friday, at last! I'm happy it's over. I ¹_____ a tiring week. OK, see you later!

MARIK Hey, where ²_____? Aren't you walking home?

CLARE No, I've got a new bike. Didn't I tell you?

MARIK No, you ³_____. When did you get that?

CLARE At the weekend. It's great! It's the ⁴_____ way to get around!

MARIK You ⁵_____ really get a helmet, Clare! If you ⁶_____, you'll hurt yourself.

CLARE I ⁷_____ fall off, don't worry. I ⁸_____ a helmet, but I just forgot it today.

MARIK Which one is your bike, then?

CLARE That blue one. It ⁹_____ quite cheap because I ¹⁰_____ afford to spend much.

MARIK It's nice. You know, I ¹¹_____ get a bike. Then we can cycle to school together.

CLARE Good idea! But you'll need to ride fast ¹²_____ with me! See you later!

1 a 've had   b was having   c 's had
2 a are you going   b do you go   c have you gone
3 a did   b not   c didn't
4 a best   b good   c better
5 a shouldn't   b may   c should
6 a fell off   b 'll fall off   c fall off
7 a don't   b won't   c mustn't
8 a bought   b 'm buying   c was buying
9 a were   b was being   c was
10 a couldn't   b can   c couldn't to
11 a might   b might not   c won't
12 a cycling   b to cycle   c for cycle

8 HIGH-FLYERS

VOCABULARY
Exceptional jobs and qualities

1 ⭐ Complete the puzzle with words for jobs and qualities. Use the clues. What's the secret word in grey?

1 He works for a company or organisation, like a bank.
2 If you have this, you don't stop until you get what you want.
3 This person has ideas to make something completely new.
4 A runner, swimmer, high-jumper, etc.
5 This doctor can perform operations.
6 This person writes music.
7 You need this to make something new and imaginative.
8 This person does experiments in a lab.
9 This person might produce books or songs.
10 With this, you can learn, understand and form opinions.
11 You can do an activity or job well if you have this.
12 A natural ability to do something well.
13 You have this if you are strong, physically or mentally.

2 ⭐⭐ Complete the sentences with words for qualities from Exercise 1.

1 It takes a lot of _____skill_____ to operate on a person's heart.
2 She won the prize for _____ for her original ideas. She's got a great imagination.
3 Maya always shows great _____ and never stops trying to do her best.
4 The _____ of a chimpanzee is similar to a human's: chimpanzees are very clever!
5 Hercules was famous for his _____. He could lift very heavy objects.

3 ⭐⭐ Complete the sentences with words for jobs from Exercise 1 and the names in the box.

> Adele   ~~Isaac Newton~~   Marie Curie
> Suzanne Collins   Tim Berners-Lee   Usain Bolt

1 _Isaac Newton_ was a _mathematician_ at Cambridge University in the 1600s.
2 The _____ of the World Wide Web is called _____.
3 _____ is the _____ of the song *Hello* from 2015.
4 _____ was a _____ who won two Nobel Prizes for important work on radioactivity.
5 _____ is a Jamaican _____ who was an Olympic champion in three different Olympic Games.
6 *The Hunger Games* series of novels is by a _____ called _____.

Explore it! 🖱️

Guess the correct answer.
Ashrita Furman has the world record for world records. He has over *100 / 200 / 300*.

Find an interesting fact about a world record. Then send a question in an email to a classmate or ask them it in the next class.

READING
Online comments

1 ☆ Read the online comments. Who has got something in common with their hero? _____

- ● ● ●

| HOME | PROFILE | BLOG | PHOTOS |

FROM EARLY CHALLENGES TO ADULT SUCCESS!

Many of you liked our article last week about young adults who faced difficult times when they were kids but never stopped trying. Comments have flown in from all over the world!

An astrophysicist when he was still a teenager, Jake Barnett has made the biggest impression on me. Doctors said he had autism when he was two, and that he might never speak. But he did, and he has shown an amazing talent for maths. Now in his 20s, Jake has an incredible memory and remembers every maths problem he has ever solved!

Hooper 30 m ago

His name is Aaron 'Wheelz' Fotheringham and he's an amazing athlete. Now an adult, he needed a wheelchair when he was eight. He wanted to do tricks like his friends on skateboards and BMXs, so he took skateboard and BMX tricks and invented his own wheelchair tricks. You need strength and determination to become an extreme sportsperson when you can't use your legs. I use a wheelchair, and Aaron's had a big effect on me.

cre8tiv 35 m ago

Bethany Hamilton was 13 and already a great surfer when a shark attacked her and bit off her left arm. Three weeks after the accident, she got back into the water and continued surfing with only one arm! She made a book deal at 14, and a movie, *Soul Surfer*, followed. Now, as an adult, Bethany works hard helping others to face their challenges.

daisymay 45 m ago

2 ★★ Read the comments again and check the meaning of these words in a dictionary. Then complete the sentences.

> ~~autism~~   extreme   face
> tricks   wheelchair

1 A child with ___autism___ might not have good communication or social skills.
2 My brother used a _____ for a while after he broke both his legs.
3 We have to _____ our problems if we want to solve them.
4 Rock climbing is exciting and dangerous – it's one of the oldest _____ sports.
5 We've learned to do some great new _____ on our skateboards.

3 ★★ Read the comments again. Are the sentences *T* (true), *F* (false) or *DS* (doesn't say)?

1 Jake has an unusual talent for remembering numbers.   T
2 He's doing research in astrophysics.   ___
3 Aaron invented new skateboard and BMX tricks.   ___
4 A lot of people watch Aaron's wheelchair tricks online.   ___
5 Bethany started surfing again three weeks after the shark attack.   ___
6 First there was a film about her, and after that she wrote a book.   ___

4 ★★★ Answer the questions with your own ideas.

1 Which person in the comments has faced the biggest challenge? Why?

_____

2 Have you faced a big challenge? What was it?

_____

LANGUAGE IN ACTION
Present perfect for experience

1 ⭐ **Complete the sentences with the present perfect form of the verb in brackets.**

1 I __'ve__ never _heard_ (hear) of Alexander Rybak.

2 A girl in my class _____ (win) a talent competition.

3 The boys _____ (have) some strange experiences.

4 She _____ (not visit) her grandparents' new house.

5 We _____ (raise) a lot of money for charity.

6 Dom _____ (ride) a bike from Land's End to John o'Groats.

2 ⭐ **Match 1–6 with a–f.**

1 Have you ever drunk   [d]
2 Which European cities   [ ]
3 Our team has won   [ ]
4 I've never read   [ ]
5 Have you ever replied   [ ]
6 We've seen their band,   [ ]

a but only on YouTube.
b to an email in English?
c has she visited?
d carrot juice?
e the book he gave me.
f the championship three times.

3 ⭐⭐ **Write questions with the present perfect. Then look at the pictures to answer them.**

1 they / ever fly in a helicopter?

A _Have they ever flown in a helicopter?_

B _No, they haven't, but they've flown on a plane._

2 they / ever swim in the sea?

A _____

B _____

3 your dad / ever make a cake?

A _____

B _____

4 ⭐⭐ **Underline and correct one mistake in each sentence.**

1 Have you ever <u>swim</u> with dolphins?
   _____ _swum_ _____

2 They never have been to England.
   _____

3 Never you have ridden a horse.
   _____

4 Have she ever broken her phone?
   _____

5 Stayed you ever in a five-star hotel?
   _____

6 I'm happy to say I have ever lost my house keys. _____

5 ⭐⭐ **Complete the email with the present perfect form of the verbs and phrases in the box.**

| be   do   ever try   ~~fly~~   never |
| explore   never surf |

● ● ●

| Mailboxes | Inbox | Sent | **New** |

Hi Harry,
How are you? I'll be in Turkey in two weeks' time! I ¹ ___'ve flown___ into Istanbul Airport before, but I ² _____ the country properly. My parents ³ _____ on lots of Turkish holidays, so in the first week they want to go to some new places. But they're also happy to revisit some of their favourite surfing beaches – they know I love the sea! I ⁴ _____ and I really want to learn. It looks a bit of an extreme sport, as it can be dangerous, but I think I'll be OK! And ⁵ _____ you _____ kite-surfing? My dad ⁶ _____ it lots of times. I'm looking forward to watching him!
Bye for now!
Ava

VOCABULARY AND LISTENING
Phrasal verbs: achievement

1 ⭐ Match the phrasal verbs with the meanings.

1	set off	d	a admire and respect someone
2	work out	☐	b act to attract attention, usually in a bad way
3	carry on	☐	c start a new business
4	look up to	☐	d leave a place to start a journey
5	give up	☐	e join in an activity or event
6	set up	☐	f calculate something to get a result
7	come up with	☐	g continue an activity or task
8	take part in	☐	h suggest or think of an idea or answer
9	show off	☐	i do what is necessary to stay equal or at the same level
10	keep up with	☐	j stop doing or having something

2 ⭐⭐ Complete the sentences with the correct form of phrasal verbs from Exercise 1. Then match them with photos (a–f).

1 Susie is excited because she _'s setting off_ on holiday. _e_
2 It was so difficult that Hector decided to _____. ☐
3 Benjie _____ his dad and wants to be like him. ☐
4 Robin always _____ to the other band members. ☐
5 My little brother is a fast runner – no one can _____ him. ☐
6 Tanya really enjoyed _____ the race. ☐

a

b

c

d

e

f

A talk

3 ⭐ Check the meaning of these words in a dictionary. Which words can you see in the photos?

> antibiotic   bacteria   mould
> Petri dish   reflect   shine

a

b

_____

_____

🎧 **4** 8.01 ⭐ Listen to the talk. What have the two discoveries got in common?

_____

🎧 **5** 8.01 ⭐⭐ Listen again and (circle) the correct options.

1 The speaker describes the inventions as happy (accidents) / experiments.
2 The 'cat's eyes' help drivers to see other drivers' lights / the middle of the road.
3 The inventor saw his car lights reflecting in part of a glass object / an animal.
4 Sir Alexander Fleming was studying bacteria / mould in a London hospital.
5 A person left the Petri dish open when Fleming was in hospital / on holiday.
6 Some mould was growing / killing the bacteria in the Petri dish.

6 ⭐⭐⭐ Choose one of the discoveries, cat's eyes or penicillin, and make notes for each heading in your notebook.

• name and nationality of the inventor
• country and place of discovery
• how the inventor discovered it
• why the discovery is important

LANGUAGE IN ACTION
Reflexive pronouns

1 ⭐ (Circle) **the correct options.**

1 Peter is always looking at (himself) / themselves in the mirror!

2 You two should prepare yourself / yourselves for the test.

3 Have you ever taught myself / yourself a new skill?

4 The cat washes yourself / itself carefully every morning.

5 We embarrassed ourselves / themselves by showing off.

6 The girls entertained themselves / herself with video games.

2 ⭐⭐ **Complete the sentences with reflexive pronouns and the correct form of the verbs in the box.**

> enter   imagine   look after   make   ~~switch off~~   teach

1 The computer screen _switches itself off_ automatically.

2 Those kids are old enough to _____ .

3 Lauren and I _____ some new yoga exercises last week.

4 He _____ for three races in our sports event: running, cycling and swimming.

5 Monica _____ a good lunch yesterday.

6 We often _____ as famous inventors.

Indefinite pronouns

3 ⭐⭐ **Put the words in the correct order to make sentences.**

1 anyone / Mars / think / has / don't / walked / I / on
   I don't think anyone has walked on Mars.

2 phone / everywhere / her / She's / for / looked
   _____

3 will / tonight / Nobody / happen / what / knows
   _____

4 nowhere / on / to / bus / was / There / sit / the
   _____

5 new / broken / has / torch / Someone / my
   _____

6 do / help / Is / anything / I / there / can / to / ?
   _____

4 ⭐ **Match 1–6 with a–f.**

1 Has anyone seen   [b]
2 Mr Kellogg invented [ ]
3 Everyone at the party [ ]
4 Olivia hasn't been   [ ]
5 I get bored when   [ ]
6 Everything was ready [ ]

a anywhere nice this summer.

b that documentary about inventors?

c I've got nothing to do.

d when the first guests arrived.

e something by accident.

f had a great time.

5 ⭐⭐ **Complete the text with the words in the box.**

> everyone   everywhere   himself
> nobody   ~~someone~~   something
> somewhere   themselves

Most of us admire [1] _someone_ who faces challenges and achieves great things. That's why [2] _____ I know looks up to the scientist Stephen Hawking. He lived [3] _____ near London until he went to Oxford University. There, he quickly proved [4] _____ to be a maths genius. However, when he was only 21, doctors told him that he had [5] _____ called motor neurone disease (MND). [6] _____ usually lives long with MND, but Hawking didn't give up and, in fact, lived another 55 years. When he couldn't walk, he used a wheelchair. Soon he lost his voice, so then he used a computerised voice to speak and write his books. He travelled [7] _____, giving talks and showing the world what people can achieve when they believe in [8] _____ .

WRITING

A competition entry

1 ⭐ **Read the advert. What do you have to do to enter the competition?**

YOUNG HEROES CLUB
ANNUAL COMPETITION

Send us your entry! Describe how you have helped someone who has faced a challenge. Tell us:

- the greatest help you have given someone
- how you did it
- what advice you have for other young helpers.

The best entry will receive a special award from a mystery celebrity!

2 ⭐ **Read the competition entry. What has Gabriela's brother achieved?**

My name is Gabriela. My brother Jamie has got learning difficulties, and he has faced many challenges.

One of my ¹_____ is helping Jamie make friends. He can't speak clearly, and because of this it's sometimes difficult for him to make new friends. At first, he became angry when I tried to help him. However, after ²_____, I've managed to bring a group of friends into Jamie's life.

How ³_____ it? First of all, I asked our parents to get Jamie a drum. He has always loved music, so he loved the drum! One day, I invited some musician friends to our house. They introduced themselves to Jamie and then just played some music. Soon Jamie started to play with them. Two of these friends have now formed a band, and Jamie is their drummer.

If you want to help someone make friends, my ⁴_____ is to find something they love doing and help them meet people with the same interest. And never give up!

3 ⭐ **Complete the competition entry with the phrases in the box.**

> advice to you   a lot of effort
> did I manage   greatest achievements

4 ⭐⭐ **Read the competition entry again and answer the questions.**

1 What challenge does Jamie face?
_____

2 What happened when his sister tried to help him?
_____

3 What did Jamie's parents buy him?
_____

4 How many people are in Jamie's band?
_____

Write a competition entry.

PLAN

5 ⭐⭐ **Make notes about how you helped a person for the competition in Exercise 1.**

1 Introduce yourself and the person you helped: _____
_____

2 Explain what you did: _____

3 Explain how you did it: _____

4 Give advice for other people: _____
_____

WRITE

6 ⭐⭐⭐ **Write your competition entry. Remember to include the present perfect, reflexive pronouns, vocabulary from this unit and phrases from the *Useful language* box (see Student's Book, p101).**

CHECK

7 **Do you ...**
- have four paragraphs?
- explain your achievement clearly?
- give useful advice?

VOCABULARY

1 Look at the pictures and (circle) the correct options.

1 *athlete / surgeon*   2 *inventor / composer*   3 *surgeon / writer*   4 *businesswoman / mathematician*

5 *athlete / scientist*   6 *composer / writer*   7 *mathematician / writer*   8 *businesswoman / athlete*

2 Put the letters in **bold** in the correct order to make words for qualities.

1 She admired the **vaiittcyre** of the architect who designed her new home. _____

2 Carlos Acosta showed great **letant** as a dancer from an early age. _____

3 Rock climbers need physical **gshtnert**. _____

4 Her **eignelelictn** was clear from the clever answers she gave. _____

5 His **ndoeittearnmi** to win made him practise for hours. _____

3 (Circle) the correct options.

1 They *set off / set up* on their journey in May 2017.

2 We all *look up to / keep up with* our teachers and listen to their advice.

3 If you want to *show off / take part in* the competition, fill in this entry form.

4 Can you help me *give up / work out* this problem?

5 Please *carry on / come up with* speaking.

6 If I don't *come up with / keep up with* a good idea soon, I'll *show off / give up*.

LANGUAGE IN ACTION

4 Complete the sentences with the present perfect form of the verbs in the box.

> be   break   hear   read   see

1 _____ you ever _____ of a mathematician called Maryam Mırzakhanı?

2 I _____ never _____ a book about astrophysics.

3 He _____ never _____ a world record, but I'm sure he will one day.

4 _____ Philip ever _____ a Studio Ghibli film?

5 _____ we _____ here before? I don't remember it.

5 Correct the <u>underlined</u> reflexive and indefinite pronouns.

1 My cat has taught <u>myself</u> to open the fridge door. _____

2 Mrs Howe is <u>nobody</u> who I've always looked up to. _____

3 Mary Ann saw <u>themselves</u> in a video clip on YouTube. _____

4 We've looked <u>anywhere</u> for our lost door keys. _____

5 You often talk to <u>ourselves</u> when you're alone. I've heard you! _____

6 I think there's <u>anything</u> wrong with my computer. _____

7 I've noticed that my brother looks at <u>herself</u> in the mirror a lot. _____

8 There was <u>anybody</u> in the house; it was empty. _____

CUMULATIVE LANGUAGE

6 Complete the conversation with the missing words. (Circle) the correct options.

JILL Oh, dear. I ¹_____ to write a 500-word essay for Mr Jenkins.

PETE I see, and you've come to me ²_____ some ideas, right?

JILL Yes, please! The title is '³_____ creative person I know'.

PETE Can't you think of ⁴_____ ?

JILL Well, ⁵_____ my Aunt Louella?

PETE I think I saw her once when she ⁶_____ with you.

JILL Maybe. She ⁷_____ us very often, but it's possible.

PETE I'll probably remember her if you ⁸_____ her.

JILL She's my mum's sister. She's ⁹_____ tall as Mum, but she's slim and blonde. Anyway, I look up to her because she's achieved a lot and she hasn't had ¹⁰_____ easy life.

PETE Really?

JILL Well, no. She was often ill as a teenager and she didn't go to university, but she taught ¹¹_____ to paint. Now she has exhibitions ¹²_____ .

PETE So, I think you have your topic, Jill, without any help from me!

1 a must	b have	c don't have
2 a getting	b and get	c to get
3 a The most	b Most	c The more
4 a nobody	b anybody	c nothing
5 a have you met ever	b have you ever met	c did you ever met
6 a is staying	b stays	c was staying
7 a doesn't visit	b don't visit	c isn't visiting
8 a may describe	b describe	c will describe
9 a not as	b more	c not the
10 a some	b any	c an
11 a herself	b her	c himself
12 a nowhere	b everywhere	c somewhere

VOCABULARY
Musical instruments and genres

1 ⭐ Put the letters in the correct order to make musical instruments and genres. Then complete the table with the words.

> ~~honroicpem~~   ~~garege~~   olivin   ssab   lkfo
> ssiclacal   ugarit   orkc   phaxosone   rumsd
> phi-oph   rpumtet   bekyarod   azjz

Instruments	Genres
microphone	reggae

2 ⭐⭐ Look at the band members (1–8) in the picture and complete the text with words from Exercise 1.

There are eight of us in our band. Bruno plays the ¹ _drums_ . We've got Janina on ² _____ and her brother Stefan plays the ³ _____ . Rob plays the ⁴ _____ and he's really good! Sally's just started to play the ⁵ _____ , but we love her and she's learning fast. Simon's a classical musician, but he plays an electric ⁶ _____ with us. He's really talented. Ramon plays the ⁷ _____ and that's Katie at the front. She's our singer, of course, and she doesn't really need that ⁸ _____ – she's got a great voice!

3 ⭐⭐ Match the photos with the musical genre words in Exercise 1.

1 ____rock____   2 _____

3 _____   4 _____

5 _____   6 _____

4 ⭐⭐ Which word in each group does not follow the same stress pattern?

1 (●) folk   bass   reggae   drums
2 (●•) reggae   guitar   trumpet   keyboard
3 (●••) violin   classical   microphone   saxophone

5 ⭐⭐⭐ Think of an example of a song or piece of music for each musical genre in Exercise 1. Use the Internet to help you if necessary.

_____
_____
_____
_____

Explore it!

Guess the correct answer.

The world's longest officially-released song is *The Rise and Fall of Bossanova*. It is about 3 / 13 / 23 hours long.

Find another interesting fact about a song. Then send a question in an email to a classmate or ask them it in the next class.

READING
An events guide

1 ⭐ Read the events guide. Do you think this is a good school party? Why / Why not?

END-OF-YEAR PARTY

Friday 4 July 7.00 pm – 10.00 pm
Ticket price: £4 online, £5 on the door

It's been a long year, but it's finally the end! Join us at the school end-of-year party in the gym. We're going to have music, dancing, food and a special guest!

7.00 pm Welcome! Feeling hungry? The school's Picnic Club will provide the evening's food: sandwiches, cakes, crisps and other yummy snacks will be available. And there will be a Super Fruit Juice Bar all evening for all you thirsty dancers!

7.30 pm DJ Quin is going to be with us with his unique mix of lights and sound. He'll be a star DJ one day, so don't miss this opportunity to dance as he plays the latest hits. He'll finish off his set with a 'Happy Half-Hour' – when he'll play any song you want!

8.30 pm You won't believe it when you see our special guest. In his solo performance he's going to tell us jokes and make us laugh (we hope!). But he isn't going to stop there: for one night only, he's also going to play the trumpet! Here's a clue: he's everyone's favourite geography teacher …

9.00 pm The evening's going to end with the band Born to be Wild. This talented family of musicians will amaze you with the number of instruments they play: bass, saxophone, drums, violin …

So, don't miss the year's best party. See you on Friday!

2 ⭐⭐ Read the events guide again and check the meaning of these words in a dictionary. Then complete the sentences.

> available ~~joke~~ latest mix provide set

1 I never know if Juan's being serious or telling a _____joke_____ .
2 The band began their _____ at eight and finished playing at nine.
3 We will _____ all the information you need for your journey.
4 Tickets for next week's concerts are now _____ online.
5 I think the _____ hit from Catfish is the best song they've ever written.
6 Tina's music is a _____ of hip-hop and reggae.

3 ⭐⭐ Read the events guide again. Answer the questions.

1 How much are tickets if you buy them before you go to the party?

2 Is the party indoors or outdoors?

3 What can the students drink?

4 What can the students do in the last 30 minutes of DJ Quin's set?

5 Why will people be surprised by the special guest?

6 What is unusual about the band Born to be Wild?

4 ⭐⭐⭐ Answer the questions with your own ideas.

1 In your opinion, which performer at the party will be the best?

2 Have you ever had an end-of-year party at school? What was it like?

LANGUAGE IN ACTION
going to

1 ⭐ **Write sentences with *going to*.**

1 I / take some photos

  I'm going to take some photos.

2 She / watch TV

  _____

3 He / not answer the phone

  _____

4 Faye / play the piano

  _____

5 They / record a song

  _____

2 ⭐⭐ **Complete the sentences with *going to* and the verbs in the box.**

> be bring not tell ~~organise~~ see

1 I *'m going to organise* a party for my best friend.

2 We _____ her anything about it.

3 Carmen _____ food and drinks to the party.

4 We _____ a folk-rock concert.

5 The party _____ in my garage.

3 ⭐⭐ **Write sentences about the people with *going to* and the phrases in the box.**

> enter a talent competition ~~get a job as a DJ~~
> get free concert tickets run a marathon study singing

1 Nasrin loves making playlists and discovering new music.

  Nasrin's going to get a job as a DJ.

2 I've always wanted to go to music college.

  _____

3 Lily dreams of becoming a comedian.

  _____

4 Finn and Livvy run and train hard every day.

  _____

5 Max and I are lucky: we have a friend in the band.

  _____

will and *going to*

4 ⭐ **Complete the sentences with *will* or *won't*.**

1 He's sure it _____will_____ be a great event because the guide looked interesting.

2 I _____ pay £150 for a ticket – that's too much.

3 Your parents _____ get angry if your music is too loud, so turn it down.

4 _____ all three sisters sing in the same band?

5 It _____ be cold at the party, so you don't need a coat.

5 ⭐⭐ **Decide if the sentences are predictions or intentions. Then ⬭circle⬭ the best options to complete the dialogues.**

1 A What ⬭are you going to⬭ / will you do this evening?

  B I'm going to / 'll see a show at the City Hall.

2 A What are you going to / will you sing? Have you decided?

  B No, but I promise you'll / 're going to like it!

3 A Elena's going to / will learn the saxophone.

  B She'll / 's going to be good at that. She's musical.

4 A The Headsets aren't going to / won't tour any more.

  B Oh, no. That won't / isn't going to be very popular with their fans.

6 ⭐⭐ **Complete the chat with the correct form of *will* or *going to* and the verbs in brackets.**

[1] ___Are___ you _going to be_ (be) at home later?

No, I [2] _____ (meet) my dad at the music shop. I've decided: I [3] _____ (ask) him to buy me the guitar I saw in the window.

Really? You know you [4] _____ (get) a better price online.

Yeah, but I [5] _____ (try) it before we buy it – that's my plan anyway.

Well, OK, but do you play the guitar?

No, I don't, but I'm sure I [6] _____ (learn) fast! It can't be that difficult.

VOCABULARY AND LISTENING A discussion
Dance styles

1 ☆ Match five of the dance styles in the box with the shoes the dancers wear.

> ~~ballet dancing~~ ballroom dancing breakdance
> country dancing disco dancing modern dance
> salsa dancing swing tap dancing Zumba

1 _ballet dancing_

2 _____

3 _____

4 _____

5 _____

2 ☆ (Circle) the correct options.

1 In the 1970s, (disco) / *ballet* dancing was a popular dance in nightclubs.

2 *Salsa* / *Tap* dancing is a type of dance from Latin America.

3 *Breakdance* / *Swing* is a strong, exciting style of jazz dancing with a partner.

4 My grandparents don't like *modern dance* / *country*. They prefer more traditional dancing styles.

5 *Swing* / *Zumba* is a type of exercise, often in a class, with dance movements.

🎧 3 9.01 ☆☆ Listen to the discussion and answer the questions.

1 How many speakers do you hear? _____

2 How many are male and how many are female?

_____

3 How many are native and how many are non-native speakers? _____

🎧 4 9.01 ☆☆ Listen again. Are the sentences *T* (true) or *F* (false)?

1 The class is going to report back on their discussion next week. _F_

2 The after-school classes start next week. ___

3 One of the teachers is planning a school musical. ___

4 Jessica wants to do modern dance. ___

5 Camila wants to do sport next term. ___

6 Enzo wants to have a PE class after school. ___

5 ☆☆☆ Answer the questions.

1 What music or dance activities can you do at your school?

_____

2 What other after-school activities or clubs does your school have?

_____

LANGUAGE IN ACTION
Present continuous for future

1 ⭐ **Complete the sentences with the present continuous form of the verbs in brackets.**

1 Our school ___'s performing___ (perform) a musical next term.

2 Katie _____ (help) with the costumes after school.

3 Ms Wilson _____ (teach) us the dance moves next week.

4 Who _____ (write) the programmes for the new musical?

5 I _____ (not play) in the orchestra next time.

6 _____ you _____ (come) to watch the show tonight?

2 ⭐ **Write sentences with the present continuous.**

1 the musicians / leave for London tomorrow
___The musicians are leaving for London tomorrow.___

2 they / perform three evening concerts in July
_____

3 a journalist / interview the lead singer later
_____

4 a TV camera operator / record tomorrow's show
_____

5 the drummer / not play with the band tonight
_____

6 he / fly to New York next week to study music
_____

3 ⭐⭐ **Complete the sentences with the present continuous form of the verbs in the box.**

| arrive   cook   ~~help~~   not come   not do   watch |

1 Jonny ___is helping___ his sister with her homework later.

2 The boys _____ a film after school.

3 I _____ pasta tonight. Who wants to come?

4 Helena's busy so she _____ to the theatre.

5 When _____ the stars of the show _____?

6 We _____ anything special tonight.

Present simple for future

4 ⭐ **Complete the sentences with the present simple form of the verbs in brackets.**

1 The next show ___starts___ (start) at eight.

2 The singers _____ (arrive) at five in the afternoon.

3 Our train _____ (leave) at six the next morning.

4 Tomorrow's rehearsal _____ (not finish) until the evening.

5 ⭐⭐ **Write questions for the answers in Exercise 4.**

1 What time ___does the next show start___?

2 When _____ ?

3 What time _____ ?

4 When _____ ?

6 ⭐⭐ ⟨Circle⟩ **the correct options.**

> **ADAM** [1]⟨Are you doing⟩ / Do you do anything this afternoon?
>
> **AVA** Yes, my big brother and I [2]meet / are meeting our cousin Greg outside the club. He [3]'s coming / comes to stay with us after his performance.
>
> **ADAM** Ah, yes – the rapper! [4]Don't you watch / Aren't you watching his show?
>
> **AVA** I've seen it twice! We [5]'re getting / get something to eat on the way home.
>
> **ADAM** What time [6]is the show finishing / does the show finish?
>
> **AVA** It [7]ends / 's ending at 7.30, so we [8]'re going / go to that new Italian place. We [9]buy / 're buying pizzas to take home for dinner!

WRITING

A review

1 ⭐ Read the review. Where is the performance taking place? _____

Eleven – the Musical! ★★★★★

This year's Year 11 students have formed a unique song and dance group. Their show, called *Eleven – the Musical!*, tells the story of Kurt Goldberg, a theatre director, and the dancers who want to perform in his show. The music is a mix of disco and swing. Some of Year 11's best musicians also play their own songs.

It's a classic story of dancers who come to the city to become famous. I was <u>very impressed</u> by the beautiful costumes and creative make-up, and Chris Randall is superb as Kurt Goldberg. However, the <u>highlight</u> of the show was the singing. Chris has a powerful voice and the dancers' songs were often funny. On the <u>downside</u>, the set was not very exciting.

Eleven – the Musical! is on again in the main hall next Friday and Saturday. After that, Chris is leaving to study opera and others in the group are continuing their theatre studies in different colleges in the UK. <u>All in all</u>, <u>if you love</u> music, this unique musical is <u>a must-see</u>.

2 ⭐ Complete the sentences with the <u>underlined</u> phrases in the review.

1 I was <u>very impressed</u> by the funny script.

2 So, _____ hip-hop, this show is for you.

3 The _____ of the show was the superb tap dancing. I loved it!

4 For anyone who enjoys jazz, this show is _____ .

5 On the _____ , the lead guitarist didn't play well.

6 _____ , it's a show you mustn't miss.

3 ⭐⭐ Which things do these adjectives describe?

1 unique   *the song and dance group*

2 classic   _____

3 beautiful   _____

4 creative   _____

5 superb   _____

6 powerful   _____

7 funny   _____

8 not exciting   _____

Write a review of a school show that you have seen or been in.

PLAN

4 ⭐⭐ Make notes about these things.

1 A general description of the show:

_____

2 Details about the dancing, music, costumes, etc. and what you liked/didn't like:

_____

3 A summary of your opinion:

_____

WRITE

5 ⭐⭐⭐ Write your review. Remember to use adjectives, the present simple to describe the show, the past simple for your opinion and phrases from the *Useful language* box (see Student's Book, p113).

CHECK

6 Do you …

• use three paragraphs?

• say what you liked and didn't like?

• summarise your opinions at the end?

VOCABULARY

1 Look at the photos and complete the descriptions below with words for musical instruments and genres.

1 Katrina plays the _____ . She has studied _____ music.

2 Bryony loves _____ music and plays the _____ in the park.

3 Marius is a great _____ artist. All he needs is his _____ to speak into.

4 Monica plays the _____ in a reggae band and Milton plays the _____.

5 Ella plays the _____ guitar and Joe plays the _____ in their band.

6 Our music teacher plays the _____ in a _____ club.

2 Find ten dance styles in the wordsnake.

discosalsatapballroombreakdancezumbaswingcountryballetmodern

LANGUAGE IN ACTION

3 Complete the email with the correct form of *going to* or *will* and the verbs in the box.

> be   bring   cost   finish   go
> have   meet   not rain

TO: Jed
FROM: Lindy

Hi Jed,

Aidan and I ¹_____ to a music festival at the weekend. Do you remember Jake and Ida? They ²_____ us there. I ³_____ all my homework first so I can really relax and enjoy myself! Aidan ⁴_____ sandwiches and hot drinks because we think the festival food ⁵_____ a lot – it's always expensive!
I hope it ⁶_____ on Friday, but I think it ⁷_____ cloudy all weekend. I'm not worried about that – I'm sure we ⁸_____ fun.

Hope your weekend's fun too!

See you soon,
Lindy

4 (Circle) the correct options.

1 I'm not doing / don't do anything special this afternoon.

2 The programme says the music starts / is starting at 8.30 pm.

3 People are arriving / arrive at seven tonight for the party.

4 Are you using / Do you use that microphone tonight?

5 Who's writing / writes the songs for next year's show?

6 The ticket office opens / is opening tomorrow at 9 am.

7 A really exciting event is happening / happens at our school next week.

8 You'll have to run for the last bus because the show isn't ending / doesn't end until 10.30.

CUMULATIVE LANGUAGE

5 Complete the conversation with the missing words. (Circle) the correct options.

> **HARRY** Have you ¹_____ of SoGood Sounds?
>
> **TINA** If they ²_____ a reggae band, I won't know them. I'm not as interested in that kind of music ³_____ you are.
>
> **HARRY** No, no, there's an organisation called SoGood Sounds. ⁴_____ of them?
>
> **TINA** No. What ⁵_____?
>
> **HARRY** They organise outdoor music festivals ⁶_____ money for charities. They're all musicians, and they raise money for disabled people because some of them can't live alone or look after ⁷_____.
>
> **TINA** Oh, I see. Do you know ⁸_____ more about the music they play?
>
> **HARRY** Not really. I think that there ⁹_____ be one of their concerts next weekend, but I'm not sure. I ¹⁰_____ to look on the website tonight.
>
> **TINA** OK, so when you get ¹¹_____ information, can you text me?
>
> **HARRY** Of course. I'll do that if I ¹²_____, no problem!

1	a heard ever	b ever heard	c ever hear
2	a are	b will be	c won't be
3	a like	b than	c as
4	a Did you hear	b Have you heard	c Were you hearing
5	a they do	b are they doing	c do they do
6	a to raise	b for raise	c for raising
7	a itself	b themselves	c theirselves
8	a anything	b anywhere	c anyone
9	a has to	b might	c might to
10	a will	b 'm going	c should
11	a an	b a	c some
12	a 'm remembering	b 'll remember	c remember

Reading: Multiple choice

You will read a long text, which is often based on a newspaper or magazine article. This exam task tests your understanding of the most important ideas and some details of the text. The title tells you what the topic is. There are five multiple-choice questions. To answer the questions you need to choose the correct answer, A, B or C.

Example:

How does Estefania feel about the school exchange trip?

A She's excited to meet new people.

B She's worried about speaking a new language.

C She's nervous about being away from home for the first time.

Exam guide: Multiple choice

- Start by reading the title of the text so you know what the topic is.

- Read the whole text quickly first to find out more about the topic and to get a general understanding.

- Read the text again more carefully to get a better understanding. Use the context to work out the meaning of any new vocabulary, but don't spend too much time worrying about unfamiliar words at this point.

- Now read all the questions carefully and underline the important 'key' words in the questions. This helps you when you look for the same information in the text.

  Example:

  How does <u>Estefania</u> <u>feel</u> about the <u>school</u> <u>exchange</u> <u>trip</u>?

- Read the first question again. Then look for the part of the text where you think you might find the answer. If you remember something from when you read through the text, go back to that part first to check. If not, read from the beginning until you find what you need.

- When you find the relevant part of the text, <u>underline</u> the words and write the number of the question next to the words you underlined. Then circle the option in the question, A, B or C, that most closely matches the meaning in the text. Use the key words in the question to help you.

  Example:

  <u>I'm really happy to go to Dublin to learn English and stay with an English-speaking family, and I don't mind being away from home, but I hope I won't forget the English I already know and I can understand everyone!</u>

- Remember to check the other two options as well to decide why they aren't correct.

- Now read the other questions and repeat the process until you finish.

- You don't lose points for a wrong answer, so always give an answer for each question even if you aren't sure.

REMEMBER!

The text often mentions information from all three options, but only one option is correct. Read the text carefully and match the meaning, not the words.

Reading practice: Multiple choice

1 <u>Underline</u> the key words in the questions.

0 <u>What</u> <u>after-school</u> <u>activities</u> does <u>Lena</u> <u>like</u> <u>doing</u> on <u>Mondays</u>?

1 What day does Tom prefer playing tennis with his brother?

2 Why does Mason think art classes are difficult?

3 Who prefers studying alone to studying with other people?

4 How did Eva feel on the morning of her exam?

5 What, according to Josh, is the best thing about eating lunch at home?

Tip!
'Key' words carry the meaning in a sentence: they are usually nouns, adjectives, verbs, adverbs and question words. Underlining these words in questions can help you to focus on the information you need to find in the text.

2 <u>Underline</u> the key words in questions 1–5. Then match 1–5 with A–E.

1 What's Ben doing with his friends now?

2 What did Ben do last weekend with his aunt?

3 Where did Ben arrange to see his friend last week?

4 What does Ben do Monday to Friday after school?

5 Where does Ben go on Saturdays?

A He met him in the park on Friday.

B He plays basketball during the week.

C Today, they're at the sports centre.

D He goes to computer club every weekend.

E On Saturday, he went to the cinema with her.

3 Choose the option, A, B or C, which has the same meaning as each sentence (1–3). Then <u>underline</u> the words and phrases which helped you to match the sentences.

Tip!
Look out for words or phrases which look different in the questions and text but have the same meaning, for example, synonyms, or antonyms with a negative verb.

0 Lily <u>hates</u> going to her grandma's after school.

(A) Lily <u>really doesn't like</u> going to her grandma's after school.

B Lily doesn't mind going to her grandma's after school.

C Lily likes going to her grandma's after school.

1 Harry was nervous about the exam results.

A Harry wasn't worried about the exam results.

B Harry felt worried about the exam results.

C Harry was excited about the exam results.

2 We were tired after the journey.

A We didn't have much energy after the journey.

B The journey was tiring, but we felt OK after it.

C We were full of energy after the journey.

3 My parents are upset with me.

A My parents aren't unhappy with me.

B My parents aren't angry with me.

C My parents aren't very happy with me.

4 Read the text and match the words in **bold** with the synonyms 1–5.

Last night our neighbours were on a game show on TV! Mr and Mrs Jackson seemed quite **worried** at the beginning of the **show** because they were losing. Mr Jackson looked **scared** and couldn't answer his questions very well, but Mrs Jackson answered her questions **with no difficulty**. The final question was for the Jackson team, and they thought about it **with care** before answering. They got the answer **right** and won the game in the end, which was fantastic!

0 nervous <u>worried</u>

1 easily _____

2 carefully _____

3 programme _____

4 correct _____

5 afraid _____

EXAM TIPS: Reading skills

Reading: Open cloze

You will complete six gaps in a short, simple text using one word only per gap. All words must be spelled correctly. This task tests your knowledge of parts of speech such as verbs, determiners, prepositions and pronouns. There is one example in the text, marked '0'.

Example:

Have you (0) _____ the new Fantastic Beasts *film?*

Exam guide: Open cloze

- First, read the text quickly to find out the topic and understand the general meaning.

- Think about the possible words that might go in the gaps as you read through.

- Look carefully at the words before and after each gap, and read the whole sentence before deciding on a suitable answer. Underline any important words.

- Remember that you must write only ONE word per gap.

- If you are not sure of an answer, move on to the next item. You can do the ones you find easiest first and come back to the more difficult ones at the end.

- For difficult items, use the words before and after the gap to try to work out the part of speech. For example, if the gap is preceded by a subject pronoun, the missing word is probably a verb. If it comes after a verb or a noun, it may be a preposition.

- If you think that more than one answer is possible, think very carefully about the sentence and the structure again. Read the sentence over in your head with both alternatives. Choose the word you feel fits best. Sometimes there is more than one possible answer, but remember you can write only ONE of these correct words in the gap.

  Example:

  *Have you (0) **seen** the new* Fantastic Beasts *film?*

  *Have you (0) **watched** the new* Fantastic Beasts *film?*

- When you have completed all the gaps, read the whole text again carefully to check your answers and spelling.

- You don't lose points for a wrong answer, so always write something for each gap. If you aren't sure, guess.

REMEMBER!

The most common parts of speech which are tested in this exam part are pronouns (e.g. *her*), determiners (e.g. *some*), conjunctions (e.g. *because*), time expressions (e.g. *since*), auxiliary verbs (e.g. *would*) and prepositions (e.g. *in*).

Reading practice: Open cloze

1 What type of word is missing in each sentence? Circle the correct parts of speech.

0 We saw _____ great film last night.   article / verb

1 Noel fell _____ his skateboard and hurt his knee.   preposition / verb

2 He bought _____ girlfriend a new pair of shoes.   preposition / possessive adjective

3 You don't _____ to come if you don't want to.   verb / determiner

4 She's put too _____ salt in the food.   determiner / conjunction

5 _____ does Lisa live?   time expression / question word

6 Let's buy Lucy a present _____ it's her birthday.   conjunction / pronoun

2 Complete the sentences in Exercise 1 with the correct missing words.

3 Read the text and correct the words in bold.

⁰**Does** you know Corey's cousin, James? He's ¹**a** athlete! He ²**win** two gold medals for ³**her** school last year, and he wants to ⁴**running** in the county championships next month. He exercises five times a week ⁵**on** the sports club, and he always tries to do ⁶**best** each time. He's ⁷**so** talented as the other athletes, and I believe he can win the championships ⁸**on** the future.

0 <u>Do</u>   2 _____   4 _____   6 _____   8 _____

1 _____   3 _____   5 _____   7 _____

4 Circle the correct missing words to complete the sentences.

0 … it rain last night?   *a* Has   *b* Did   *c* Was

1 I can't do this question. It's … hard!   a too   b enough   c as

2 Kerry did very … in the exams.   a good   b bad   c well

3 The alarm went off … our maths class.   a at   b during   c while

4 You … run in the school corridors.   a don't   b must   c shouldn't

5 Were you … to call me just now?   a trying   b tried   c try

5 Match one word from each box with each gap.

can   ~~if~~   need   on   very   what

could   have   off   really   ~~when~~   which

0 … you heat ice, it melts.   <u>If</u>   <u>When</u>

1 I thought I did badly in the test, but I got a … good score!   _____ _____

2 … country did you go to on holiday?   _____ _____

3 We … to get to the station by ten o'clock to catch the train.   _____ _____

4 … you open the window, please?   _____ _____

5 Do you know how to turn … this computer?   _____ _____

EXAM TIPS: Listening skills

Listening: Matching

You will listen to a conversation between two people who know each other and match information in two lists of items. You will hear the conversation twice. This exam task tests your understanding of detailed information. Before you listen to the conversation, you will hear instructions explaining who is speaking and what they are talking about.

Example:

*You will hear **Josh and Stella** talking about **the band for a new school musical**.*

To complete the task, you need to match the items in the first list with the correct items in the second list. There are five items in the first list and eight in the second: there are three extra items you don't need.

Example:

You will hear Josh and Stella talking about the band for a new school musical. Which musical instrument is each person going to play?

1	Josh	A	bass guitar
2	Stella	B	drums
3	Kristie	C	guitar
4	Ella	D	keyboard
5	Adam	E	piano
		F	saxophone
		G	trumpet
		H	violin

Exam guide: Matching

- You will have time before you listen to read the question and look at the lists. Read them carefully and think about the context so you know what you can expect to hear.

- You will see that all the words in each list belong to the same vocabulary group. The first list is usually people and the second list is a group of nouns such as sports, food or musical instruments. In the recording you will hear the items in the first list in the same order in which they appear on the page.

- When you listen the first time, try and understand the general meaning of the conversation and think about the best option for each answer. If you aren't sure, don't worry. The second time you listen you can check your first answer or make another choice.

- The first time you listen, you can also try to identify the items in the second list that are not needed. You can then cross these out so you can focus only on the other items when you listen the second time.

- When you listen the second time, focus more on specific information and check your answers carefully.

- You don't lose points for a wrong answer, so always write an answer for each item. If you aren't sure, guess.

REMEMBER!

It's important to know when to stop focusing on a question you're not sure about, so that you don't miss the next question. Don't spend too long on one item – try and follow the conversation. You can revise your answers when you listen the second time or at the end of the task.

Listening practice: Matching

E.01 1 Read the instruction and question, and answer the questions below. Then listen and check your ideas.

You will hear Josh and Stella talking about the band for a new school musical. Which musical instrument is each person going to play?

1 Why do you think they're talking about the band for the school musical?

_____

2 What kinds of words do you think you will hear in the conversation?

_____

3 Where do you think they are having their conversation?

_____

E.02 2 Listen to the conversations. Which item is mentioned but <u>isn't</u> the correct answer in each conversation? Put a cross (✗) next to the incorrect options.

1 Sally enjoys watching …   a comedies. ☐   b dramas. ✗   c soap operas. ☐

2 For the picnic, Joe needs to bring …   a a cake. ☐   b fruit. ☐   c sandwiches. ☐

3 Pippa wants to volunteer as a …   a nurse. ☐   b carer. ☐   c paramedic. ☐

4 For sports day, Marcus is going to compete in …   a swimming. ☐   b tennis. ☐   c volleyball. ☐

5 Jessie's favourite subject is …   a maths. ☐   b science. ☐   c geography. ☐

3 Look at the lists of words (a–d). Which vocabulary group does each list belong to?

1 Where did Martin go on Saturday?

   a swimming pool   b park   c theatre   d restaurant   _places in a town_

2 What did Monica's grandfather do when he was younger?

   a paramedic   b police officer   c vet   d firefighter   _____

3 What did Tim have after his accident?

   a bruises   b a cut head   c a broken leg   d a sprain   _____

4 How does Luke get to school?

   a bus   b on foot   c car   d bike   _____

5 What things has Mina got in her bedroom?

   a armchair   b cupboard   c desk   d wardrobe   _____

E.03 4 Listen and ⟨choose⟩ the correct options in Exercise 3. You will hear all the options (a–d) mentioned in each conversation, but only two are correct.

LANGUAGE REFERENCE

Present simple

Affirmative	Negative
I / You / We / They play the piano.	I / You / We / They do not (don't) play the piano.
He / She / It plays the piano.	He / She / It does not (doesn't) play the piano.

- We use the present simple to talk about facts, habits and routines.
  I speak Italian.   He goes to university.
- The third person form (*he / she / it*) of the present simple ends in **-s**.
  eat – he eats   read – she reads
- With verbs ending in **consonant** + **-y**, we replace the **-y** with **-ies** for the *he / she / it* forms.
  study – she studies
- The *he / she / it* form of verbs ending in **-ss**, **-sh**, **-ch**, **-x** and **-o** is **-es**.
  kisses finishes teaches relaxes goes
- Some verbs have got an irregular spelling in the third person.
  have – she has   be – he is
- We form the negative of the present simple with the **subject** + **don't**/**doesn't** + **infinitive**.
  They don't speak Italian.
- We use **doesn't** in the third person (*he / she / it*).
  He doesn't play in the school team.

Question	Short answer
Do I / you / we / they like rugby?	Yes, I / you / we / they do. No, I / you / we / they don't.
Does he / she / it like rugby?	Yes, he / she / it does. No, he / she / it doesn't.

- We form present simple **Yes**/**No** questions with **do**/**does** + **subject** + **infinitive**.
  Do you read magazines?
- We use short answers with **do**/**does** to reply. We don't repeat the main verb.
  A Do you write a blog? B Yes, I do. (NOT ~~Yes, I write~~.)

Adverbs of frequency

always   usually   often   sometimes   never

100% ←——————————————————→ 0%

- Adverbs of frequency say how often we do something. They go after the verb **be** but before all other verbs.
  She's always late.   He sometimes chats online.
- In questions, adverbs of frequency always come after the subject.
  Do you always watch TV online?

love, like, don't mind, hate + -ing

- We use the **-ing** form of the verb after **like**, **don't like**, **don't mind**, **love** and **hate**.
  She loves making cakes. (NOT ~~She loves make cakes~~.)
- We can also use nouns after these verbs.
  He doesn't mind basketball, but he loves athletics.

have got

Affirmative	Negative
I / You / We / They have ('ve) got a phone.	I / You / We / They have not (haven't) got a phone.
He / She / It has ('s) got a phone.	He / She / It has not (hasn't) got a phone.

- We use **have got** to talk about possession and relationships.
  I've got five brothers.
- We usually use contractions in conversation.
  He's got an uncle in the UK.
- We use the full form of the verb **have got** to be more formal.
  He has got an uncle in the UK.
- To make the negative, we put **n't** (*not*) after **have** and before **got**.
  We haven't got a portable charger.

Question	Short answer
Have I / you / we / they got a laptop?	Yes, I / you / we / they have. No, I / you / we / they haven't.
Has he / she / it got a laptop?	Yes, he / she / it has. No, he / she / it hasn't.

- We use **have** + **subject** + **got** + **object** in questions.
  Have you got headphones?
- In spoken English, we reply to questions with short answers.
  A Have you got a tablet?
  B Yes, I have. (NOT ~~Yes, I have got~~.) / No, I haven't. (NOT ~~No, I haven't got~~.)

LANGUAGE PRACTICE

Present simple

1 Complete the table with the third person form of the verbs in the box.

> fly   get up   go   ~~play~~   try   watch

-s	-es	-ies
1 _plays_	3 _____	5 _____
2 _____	4 _____	6 _____

2 Complete the sentences with the present simple form of the verbs in brackets.

1 Marta and Matt ___like___ sport. (like)
2 I do my homework during the week, but my best friend _____ it on a Sunday. (do)
3 They _____ hockey on Saturdays. (play)
4 My sister _____ English at university. (study)
5 My dad _____ the bus to work every day. (catch)

3 Write sentences with the present simple.

1 I / not like / athletics
   I don't like athletics.
2 Harry / read / the school magazine / every week
   _____
3 My sister / not hang out / with friends in the evening
   _____
4 My friends / love / my new blog
   _____
5 Laura and Dan / not play / hockey on Saturdays
   _____
6 We / do / homework / at the homework club
   _____

4 Write *Yes/No* questions and short answers.

1 Molly / get up / at 6 am / every day / ? (✓)
   Does Molly get up at 6 am every day?   _Yes, she does._
2 Dan / read / your blog / ? (✗)
   _____   _____
3 you / play computer games / with your friends / ? (✓)
   _____   _____
4 your sister / write / good stories / ? (✗)
   _____   _____
5 Rabia and Fatima / go to / the same school / ? (✓)
   _____   _____

Adverbs of frequency

5 Circle the correct options.

1 Dan *always does* / *does always* his homework in front of the TV.
2 They *often are* / *are often* in the park at the weekend.
3 Gina and Martin *usually go* / *go usually* to the cinema on Saturdays.
4 I *sometimes get* / *get sometimes* DVDs from the library.
5 My sister *never is* / *is never* late for school.
6 Alex *usually listens* / *listens usually* to music in the evening.

love, like, don't mind, hate + -ing

6 Write sentences with *love, like, don't mind, hate + -ing*.

1 I / love / watch / films
   I love watching films.
2 Molly / not mind / get up / early
   _____
3 We / like / go / to the cinema
   _____
4 My dad / hate / listen / to the radio
   _____
5 Rosie / not mind / do / homework
   _____

have got

7 Complete the text with the correct form of *have got*. Use contractions.

I [1] _'ve got_ a new friend in my class. Her name's Maria. She [2] _____ brown hair and blue eyes. She [3] _____ (not) any brothers, but she [4] _____ three sisters. Her mum and dad [5] _____ a house next to ours! I really like her because we [6] _____ the same hobbies and we like the same things! What about you? [7] _____ you _____ a good friend in your class? [8] _____ your friend _____ the same hobbies as you?

Present continuous

Affirmative	Negative
I am ('m) watching TV.	I am ('m) not watching TV.
You / We / They are ('re) watching TV.	You / We / They are not (aren't) watching TV.
He / She / It is ('s) watching TV.	He / She / It is not (isn't) watching TV.

- We use the present continuous to talk about actions in progress at the time of speaking.
  You are learning about the present continuous.
- For the affirmative, we use **subject** + *be* + **verb** + *-ing*.
  Tom's watching a reality show. We're reading a blog.
- For the negative, we put *not* after *be*.
  She is not (isn't) downloading songs.

Question	Short answer
Am I watching TV?	Yes, I am. No, I'm not.
Are you / we / they watching TV?	Yes, you / we / they are. No, you / we / they aren't.
Is he / she / it watching TV?	Yes, he / she / it is. No, he / she / it isn't.

- To form questions, we use *be* + **subject** + **verb** + *-ing*.
  Are you watching cartoons?
- We don't use the **verb** + *-ing* in short answers.
  Yes, I am. (NOT *Yes, I am listening.*)
- We form information questions with the *Wh-* question word before *be*.
  Who are you reading about?
  What are you watching on TV?
- With most verbs, we add *-ing* to the infinitive.
  speak – speaking   read – reading   drink – drinking
- For verbs ending in *-e*, we remove the *-e* and add *-ing*.
  write – writing   have – having   give – giving
- For verbs ending in a vowel and a consonant, we double the final consonant and add *-ing*.
  stop – stopping   shop – shopping   plan – planning

Present simple and present continuous

- We use the present simple to talk about facts, habits and routines.
  Water freezes at 0 °C.
  I listen to music when I walk to school.
  She always goes shopping on Fridays.
- We use the present continuous to talk about actions in progress at the time of speaking.
  I watch a lot of TV. At the moment, I'm watching a great on-demand series.
  He usually works in an office, but he's working at home today.
- Some verbs are not usually used in the continuous form: *hate, know, like, love, need, prefer, remember, think, understand, want.*
  I like this programme. (NOT *I'm liking this programme.*)
- We use expressions like *at the moment* and *right now* with the present continuous.
  He's doing his homework at the moment.
- We use adverbs of frequency with the present simple.
  He always does his homework after dinner.

Adverbs of manner

- We use adverbs of manner to say how we do something.
  Carl can run very fast.
- Adverbs of manner come after the verb or the object if the sentence contains one.
  They don't speak clearly.
  Lia can draw animals well.
- To form regular adverbs we add *-ly* to the adjective.
  nice – nicely   loud – loudly
- For adjectives ending in *-y*, we remove the *-y* and add *-ily*.
  happy – happily   noisy – noisily
- For adjectives ending in *-l*, we add *-ly*.
  careful – carefully   beautiful – beautifully
- Some adverbs of manner are irregular.
  good – well   hard – hard   late – late

LANGUAGE PRACTICE

Present continuous

1 Complete the table with the *-ing* form of the verbs in the box.

| do | run | take | travel | walk | write |

add *-ing*	remove the -e and add -ing	double the consonant and add -ing
1 _doing_	3 _____	5 _____
2 _____	4 _____	6 _____

2 Complete the sentences with the present continuous form of the verbs in brackets.

1 My best friends _are reading_ in the library. (read)

2 I _____ for a new camera. (look)

3 My mum _____ in the café. (sit)

4 She _____ coffee. (not drink)

5 My dad _____ a chocolate cake in the kitchen. (make)

6 Rosie and Dan _____ online. (not chat)

3 Write present continuous questions and short answers about the people in the table.

	watch a film	study grammar
Jack	(1) ✗	(4) ✓
Rory and Holly	(2) ✓	(5) ✗
Alba	(3) ✗	(6) ✓

1 _Is Jack watching a film?_
No, he isn't.

2 _____

3 _____

4 _____

5 _____

6 _____

Present simple and present continuous

4 Put the words in the correct order to make sentences in the present simple or present continuous.

1 isn't / She / documentary / watching / the
She isn't watching the documentary.

2 makes / My mum / always / for the show / the costumes
_____

3 English / We / studying / aren't / today
_____

4 to / the / best friend / to go / doesn't / want / cinema / My
_____

5 weekend / I / to / friends / at / the / chat / my / online
_____

6 moment / I'm / helping / my / mum / the / at
_____

5 Complete the sentences with the present simple or present continuous form of the verbs in the box.

| listen | make | not do | not talk | visit | watch |

1 We _'re watching_ a comedy show right now.

2 I _____ my homework at the moment.

3 They often _____ their aunt on Saturdays.

4 My grandma usually _____ to the news on the radio in the morning.

5 My mum sometimes _____ the food we see on cookery shows.

6 Jack _____ on his mobile phone to his best friend at the moment.

Adverbs of manner

6 Complete the text with the adverb form of the adjectives in brackets.

My brother doesn't make friends [1] _easily_ (easy). He's only got two really good friends. They usually play computer games at home. I don't play with them because they do everything really [2]_____ (quick), and I play [3]_____ (slow) and [4]_____ (bad)!
My brother loves drawing and he can draw [5]_____ (good). Sometimes he teaches me how to draw. I think he's a good teacher because he explains everything [6]_____ (careful).

Past simple

Affirmative	Negative
I / You / He / She / It / We / They went to a museum.	I / You / He / She / It / We / They did not (didn't) go to a museum.
be	
I / He / She / It was bored.	I / He / She / It was not (wasn't) bored.
You / We / They were bored.	You / We / They were not (weren't) bored.

- We use the past simple to talk about completed events and actions in the past.
  He watched a history documentary last night.
  We were tired after the journey.
- Most verbs in the past simple end in **-ed**.
  want – wanted   need – needed   show – showed
- For verbs ending in **-e**, add **-d**.
  live – lived   hate – hated   phone – phoned
- For verbs ending **consonant** + **-y**, we remove the **-y** and add **-ied**.
  study – studied   carry – carried   marry – married
- For verbs ending **consonant** + **vowel** + **consonant**, we double the final consonant and add **-ed**.
  shop – shopped   travel – travelled   stop – stopped
- Some past simple verbs are irregular.
  become – became   come – came   put – put
- See the irregular verbs list on page 111.
- To form the past simple negative, we use **subject** + **did not (didn't)** + **infinitive** without **to**.
  Borja didn't finish his homework last night.
- To form the past simple negative of **be**, add **not (n't)**.
  Mum wasn't very happy about my exam results.

Question	Short answer
Did I / you / he / she / it / we / they go to a museum?	Yes, I / you / he / she / it / we / they did. No, I / you / he / she / it / we / they didn't.
be	
Was I / he / she / it bored?	Yes, I / he / she / it was. No, I / he / she / it wasn't.
Were you / we / they bored?	Yes, you / we / they were. No, you / we / they weren't.

- To form past simple questions, we use **Did** + **subject** + **infinitive** without **to**.
  Did Tom enjoy the concert yesterday?
- We put question words before **did**.
  What did you do last weekend?
- To form past questions with **be**, change the word order.
  Were you late to class this morning?

there was/there were

	Affirmative	Negative
Singular	There was a bowl / some food.	There was not (wasn't) a bowl / any food.
Plural	There were some forks.	There were not (weren't) any forks.

- We use **there was** and **there were** to talk about what existed in the past.
- We use **there was** with singular countable and uncountable nouns.
  There was a book here.   There was milk in the cup.
- We use **there were** with plural countable nouns.
  There were a lot of tourists in our town last weekend.
- We use **some** after **there was**/**were** with uncountable and plural countable nouns.
  There was some water in the bottle.
  There were some houses here years ago.
- We use **any** after **there wasn't**/**weren't** with uncountable and plural countable nouns.
  There wasn't any money in the purse.
  There weren't any cups.

	Question	Short answer
Singular	Was there a bowl / any food?	Yes, there was. No, there wasn't.
Plural	Were there any forks?	Yes, there were. No, there weren't.

- In questions, we usually use **any** with uncountable and plural countable nouns.
  Was there any bread at home?
  Were there any interesting objects at the museum?
- We don't repeat **any** in short answers.
  A   *Was there any news about Laura?*
  B   *No, there wasn't* (NOT ~~No, there wasn't any.~~)

LANGUAGE PRACTICE

Past simple

1 Complete the table with the past simple form of the verbs in the box.

> cry   like   plan   smile   stay   stop   tidy   ~~wait~~

add -ed	ending in -e, add -d	remove -y, add -ied	double final consonant, add -ed
1 _waited_	3 _____	5 _____	7 _____
2 _____	4 _____	6 _____	8 _____

2 Write sentences with the past simple.

1 Tom / wait / three hours / for the train
   Tom waited three hours for the train.

2 Joanna / not go / to school / last week
   _____

3 Rosie and Sarah / not feel / tired after the journey
   _____

4 The journey / take / ten hours!
   _____

5 I / buy / some / new shoes
   _____

3 Write past simple questions and short answers about the people in the table.

	Holly	Maria and Sam	Ivan
go cinema	(1) ✗	(2) ✓	(3) ✓
eat pizza	(4) ✓	(5) ✗	(6) ✗

1 _Did Holly go to the cinema?_
   No, she didn't.

2 _____

3 _____

4 _____

5 _____

6 _____

4 Complete the question for each answer.

1 A What _did you drink?_____
  B I drank some cola.

2 A Where_____?
  B He went to a concert.

3 A When_____?
  B They started school in January.

4 A Who_____?
  B She met her sister.

5 A What_____?
  B He ate a hot dog.

6 A Why_____?
  B They stayed at home because it was foggy.

there was/there were

5 Complete the text with *there was(n't)/there were(n't)*.

When I was at primary school ¹ _there weren't_ a lot of exams and ² _____ a lot of students in my class – I think ³ _____ only nine or ten of us. In my classroom ⁴ _____ an internet connection or an electronic board, but it was beautiful. ⁵ _____ pictures and stories on the walls and ⁶ _____ a storytelling hour every day. ⁷ _____ any computers or laptops in our class, but we loved writing on the little green board!

6 ⟨Circle⟩ the correct options.

1 Were there *a / some /* ⟨*any*⟩ posters on the walls?

2 There wasn't *an / some / any* exam every week.

3 There weren't *a / some / any* computers.

4 Was there *a / some / any* board in the classroom?

5 There wasn't *a / some / any* window in the classroom.

6 There were *an / some / any* interesting storybooks.

7 Complete the questions with *Was there* or *Were there*.

1 _Were there_ many people at the party?

2 _____ any good TV programmes on last night?

3 _____ a party at your house last night?

4 _____ an exam at school last week?

5 _____ three or four students in the library?

LANGUAGE REFERENCE

Past continuous: affirmative and negative

Affirmative	Negative
I / He / She / It was travelling.	I / He / She / It was not (wasn't) travelling.
You / We / They were travelling.	You / We / They were not (weren't) travelling.

- We use the past continuous to talk about actions in progress at a specific time in the past, or actions interrupted by another action.
  We were doing homework at 5 pm yesterday.
  Chloe was reading when James texted her.
- We form affirmative sentences with **subject** + *was/were* + **verb** + *-ing*.
  He was walking to school.
- To form the negative, we put *n't* (*not*) after *was/were* and before the **verb** + *-ing*. *Not* is usually contracted.
  They weren't listening to the teacher.

Past continuous: questions

Question	Short answer
Was I / he / she / it travelling?	Yes, I / he / she / it was. No, I / he / she / it wasn't.
Were you / we / they travelling?	Yes, you / we / they were. No, you / we / they weren't.

- We form questions with *Was/Were* + **subject** + **verb** + *-ing*.
  Were you reading in bed last night?
- We don't use **verb** + *-ing* in short answers.
  A *Was he chatting online?*
  B *Yes, he was.* (NOT ~~Yes, he was chatting.~~)
- For information questions, we put the *Wh-* question word before *be*.
  What were you doing this morning?

Past simple and past continuous

- We often use the past simple and past continuous together. We use the past simple for shorter actions which interrupt longer actions in the past continuous.

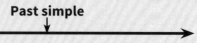

Past continuous

I was cycling to school when I saw Lily.
He was walking through the park when he fell and hurt his knee.

- We often use *when*, *while* and *as* with the past continuous.
  Their computer broke when they were studying.
  While she was having breakfast, she got a text from Madeline.
  As we were leaving the party, Lucas arrived.
- We use *when* with the past simple for shorter actions.
  When I saw Tom, he was arguing with Adele in the street.
  (NOT ~~While I saw Tom …~~)

LANGUAGE PRACTICE

Past continuous: affirmative and negative

1 Complete the sentences with the past continuous form of the verbs in the box.

> chat   get   have   hide   ~~play~~   watch

At 5 pm yesterday afternoon …

1 Peter ___was playing___ the piano.
2 Jack _____ a shower.
3 Rosie and Dan _____ to friends.
4 We _____ a drama series on TV.
5 My sister _____ dressed.
6 The children _____ under the bed!

2 Complete the sentences with the negative past continuous form of the verbs in brackets.

1 Peter ___wasn't playing___ football. (play)
2 Jack _____ emails. (write)
3 Rosie and Dan _____ in the garden. (sit)
4 We _____ our bikes. (ride)
5 I _____ a sandwich. (eat)
6 The children _____ any noise. (make)

Past continuous: questions

3 Write questions with the past continuous.

1 What / you / do / yesterday / ?
  What were you doing yesterday?
2 Where / they / go / last night / ?
  _____
3 Who / she / talk to / ?
  _____
4 Why / he / laugh / at me / ?
  _____
5 Where / you and your mum / stay / ?
  _____
6 What / your / friends / say / ?
  _____

4 (Circle) the correct options.

1 A Was he reading the story?
  B Yes, he (was) / were.
2 A Were they playing football at 4 pm?
  B No, they was / weren't.
3 A Were you talking on the phone to your friend at 10 pm last night?
  B No, I wasn't / weren't.
4 A Was your mum making breakfast at 7 am?
  B Yes, she was / were.
5 A Were you watching TV at 9 pm yesterday?
  B Yes, we was / were.
6 A Was Susan doing her homework at 6 pm?
  B Yes, she was / were.

Past simple and past continuous

5 Complete each sentence with the past simple or the past continuous form of the verbs in brackets.

1 While we ___were walking___ (walk) home we _____saw_____ (see) eight or nine cats crossing the road!
2 He _____ (go) to bed when the phone _____ (ring).
3 I _____ (fall) over while I _____ (walk) to school.
4 When I _____ (arrive) home, my dad _____ (dance) in the kitchen!
5 In the story, the man _____ (steal) the money when the police _____ (arrive).
6 While I _____ (chat) online, my mum _____ (come) into my room to turn the light off.

6 Complete the story with the past simple or the past continuous form of the verbs in brackets.

I ¹ ___was getting___ (get) into bed last night when I ² _____ (see) a light in the garden. While I ³ _____ (go) downstairs, I ⁴ _____ (hear) someone at the door! I ⁵ _____ (try) to close the door when my dad ⁶ _____ (shout), 'Let me in! It's me, your dad!'

could

Affirmative	Negative
I / You / He / She / It / We / They could swim.	I / You / He / She / It / We / They could not (couldn't) swim.

- We use **could/couldn't** to talk about ability and possibility and to ask for permission in the past.
  When I was four I could swim ten metres.
  He couldn't call earlier because he was at work.
- **Could** is the same for all persons. The third person (*he / she / it*) form doesn't end in **-s**.
  She could sing Happy Birthday in three languages.
- To form the negative, we put **n't** (**not**) after **could**.
  He couldn't pay for his university books.

Question	Short answer
Could I / you / he / she / it / we / they swim?	Yes, I / you / he / she / it / we / they could. No, I / you / he / she / it / we / they couldn't.

- To form questions, we change the order of **could** and the subject.
  Could you speak English in primary school?

Comparative and superlative adjectives

Comparatives	
Short adjectives: *smart*	add **-er**: *smarter*
Short adjectives ending in vowel + consonant: *big*	double the final consonant and add **-er**: *bigger*
Adjectives ending in -e: *safe*	add **-r**: *safer*
Adjectives ending in -y: *easy*	remove the -y and add **-ier**: *easier*
Long adjectives: *interesting*	put **more** before the adjective: *more interesting*
Irregular adjectives *good bad*	*better worse*

- We use comparative adjectives to compare one thing or person with another.
- We use the verb **be** + **comparative adjective** + **than**.
  Riley is taller than Amelia.

Superlatives	
Short adjectives: *smart*	add **-est**: *the smartest*
Short adjectives ending in vowel + consonant: *big*	double the final consonant and add **-est**: *the biggest*
Adjectives ending in -e: *safe*	add **-st**: *the safest*
Adjectives ending in -y: *easy*	remove the -y and add **-iest**: *the easiest*
Long adjectives: *interesting*	put **the most** before the adjective: *the most interesting*
Irregular adjectives *good bad*	*the best the worst*

- We use superlative adjectives to say a thing or person has got the most of a particular quality.
- We use **the** with a **superlative adjective**.
  Riley is the tallest person in her family.

too, too much, too many

- We use **too**, **too much** and **too many** to say that there is an excess of something.
- We use **too** with **adjectives**.
  I'm too excited to sleep – it's my birthday tomorrow!
- We use **too much** with **uncountable nouns**.
  I've got too much homework so I can't go out tonight.
- We use **too many** with **plural countable nouns**.
  Daniel's got too many plans for the weekend – he doesn't know which one to choose.

(not) enough + noun

- We use **enough** when we have the right amount of something or something is sufficient.
  My brother has got enough experience to work there.
- We use **not enough** when we need more of something or something is insufficient.
  I haven't got enough time to do charity work at the weekend.

LANGUAGE PRACTICE

could

1 **Complete the sentences with *could* or *couldn't* and the verb in brackets.**

1 I ___could speak___ French when I was five. (speak)

2 She _____ a shower because there wasn't any water. (not have)

3 My grandparents _____ a house when they were young because they were poor. (not buy)

4 Jack _____ all the questions in his English exam because they were easy. (answer)

5 We _____ him because he spoke very quietly. (not hear)

6 Lynn _____ a bike when she was six, but I couldn't. (ride)

2 **Put the words in the correct order to make questions with *could*.**

1 five / read / Could / were / you / when / you / ?
Could you read when you were five?

2 his / brother / Could / Spanish / speak / ?
_____

3 his / understand / Maria and David / accent / Could / ?
_____

4 six / Mason / skate / was / he / when / Could / ?
_____

5 yesterday / you / understand / Could / science / the / class / ?
_____

Comparative and superlative adjectives

3 **Complete the sentences with the comparative form of the adjectives in brackets.**

1 Maths is ___more boring___ (boring) than history.

2 Ava's homework is _____ (good) than Tim's homework.

3 Our new house is _____ (big) than the old one.

4 The weather in December is _____ (bad) than the weather in August.

5 I think my brother is _____ (intelligent) than me.

4 (Circle) **the correct options.**

1 A I think being a firefighter is *more dangerous* / (*the most dangerous*) job in the world!

B I don't agree. I think a police officer's job is *more dangerous* / *the most dangerous* than a firefighter's job.

2 A What is the *best* / *better* way to travel?

B People think it's travelling by plane, but I think going by train is *better* / *the best* than travelling by plane.

3 A I think history is *easier* / *the easiest* subject.

B I don't agree. I think science is *easier* / *the easiest* than history.

too, too much, too many; (not) enough + noun

5 **Put the words in the correct order to make sentences.**

1 to / go / to / I'm / too / park / busy / the
I'm too busy to go to the park.

2 work / My / too / dad / has / much
_____

3 clothes / got / I've / too / in / many / wardrobe / my
_____

4 enough / haven't got / money / I / buy / to / a / myself / new laptop
_____

5 hasn't got / enough / to / study / She / time
_____

6 **Complete the text with the words in the box.**

enough   not enough   too (x2)
too many   too much

I went to my first concert last week. I didn't like it. It was [1] ___too___ noisy and there were [2] _____ people there. I wanted to have something to eat, but there was [3] _____ food for everybody. After two hours I was [4] _____ hungry to stay and I asked my mum to take me home. When we arrived home, Dad had [5] _____ work and didn't have [6] _____ time to cook dinner, so we had a pizza and then I went to bed!

(*not*) as + adjective + *as*

- We use (*not*) *as* … *as* to compare one thing or person with another.
  This tablet is as expensive as a laptop.

- We use *not as* + **adjective** + *as* to say that two things or people are not equal in some way.
  Being a carer isn't as dangerous as being a firefighter.
  (= Being a firefighter is more dangerous than being a carer.)

- We use *as* + **adjective** + *as* to say two things or people are the same.
  Being a nurse is as hard as being a doctor. (= Being a doctor is as hard as being a nurse.)

(*not*) + adjective + *enough*

- We use *not* + **adjective** + *enough* when we need more of something or something is insufficient.
  I'm not old enough to work there. You need to be 16 and I'm only 15.

- We use **adjective** + *enough* when we have the right amount of something or something is sufficient.
  This carpet is big enough to cover the floor.

have to/don't have to

Affirmative	Negative
I / You / We / They have to do the ironing.	I / You / We / They do not (don't) have to do the ironing.
He / She / It has to do the ironing.	He / She / It does not (doesn't) have to do the ironing.

- We use *have to* to say that something is necessary.
  My sister has to empty the dishwasher every day.
  You have to drive on the right side of the road in Turkey.

- We use *don't have to* to say that something isn't necessary.
  I don't have to help at home, but it makes my parents happy.
  They don't have to do after-school activities at their school.

Question	Short answer
Do I / you / we / they have to do the ironing?	Yes, I / you / we / they do. No, I / you / we / they don't.
Does he / she / it have to do the ironing?	Yes, he / she / it does. No, he / she / it doesn't.

- To form questions, we use *Do/Does* + **subject** + *have to* + **infinitive**.
  Does your mum have to work at the weekend?

- In short answers we repeat *do* or *does*, not *have to*.
  A *Do you have to go to bed early during the week?*
  B *Yes, I do.* (NOT ~~Yes, I have to.~~)

LANGUAGE PRACTICE

(not) as + adjective + as

1 Complete the second sentence so it has the same meaning as the first sentence. Use (not) as + … + as and the adjectives in brackets.

1 Her new computer is smaller than her old computer.

Her old computer _isn't as small as_ her new computer. (small)

2 This red carpet is the same size as the blue one.

This red carpet _____ the blue one. (big)

3 This chest of drawers is prettier than my wardrobe.

My wardrobe _____ this chest of drawers. (beautiful)

4 These armchairs are the same price as the chairs.

The chairs _____ the armchairs. (expensive)

5 This camera is lighter than my phone.

My phone _____ this camera. (light)

6 The rooms in our apartment are wider than the rooms in your apartment.

The rooms in your apartment _____ the rooms in our apartment. (wide)

(not) + adjective + enough

2 Match 1–5 with a–e.

1 My bedroom is too small. ☐ d
2 You're too young. ☐
3 My shoes are too dirty. ☐
4 This game is too easy. ☐
5 It's too cold to go swimming. ☐

a It isn't difficult enough.
b You're not old enough.
c The weather isn't hot enough.
d It isn't big enough.
e They're not clean enough!

3 Complete the text with the phrases in the box.

> as big as   as comfortable as   as small as
> ~~as wide as~~   big enough

I got a new bed last week because I wanted a big, comfortable bed that was ¹ _as wide as_ my parents' bed. We bought one that was ² _____ for five people to sleep in! My bedroom isn't ³ _____ my parents' room (theirs is huge) and it's also smaller than my brother's, so my new bed is too big for my room really. I sleep well in the bed because it's ⁴ _____ my parents' bed, but I can't have any furniture in my room now! My brother wants to have the new bed because he says his room isn't ⁵ _____ mine, so there's more space! No way!

have to/don't have to

4 Complete the sentences with the correct form of have to.

1 My teacher _has to_ correct a lot of homework. ✓
2 To send a text message, you _____ have a phone. ✓
3 My brother _____ go to school by bus because my dad takes him in the car. ✗
4 Dan and Maria _____ do a lot of homework at the weekend. ✗
5 They _____ wear a uniform at my sister's school. ✓
6 We _____ cook dinner on Mondays and Fridays because Dad does it. ✗

5 ⊙Circle the correct options.

1 Jake has to /(doesn't have to) wash the dishes because there's a dishwasher.
2 Do / Does Cindy and Tim have to clean the bathroom?
3 Kim has to / doesn't have to do the shopping because her mum is too busy.
4 Olly has to / doesn't have to wash his own clothes because there is a washing machine.
5 Mum and Dad don't have to / have to clean the kitchen because we do it.
6 **A** Do / Does Lauren have to do any chores at home?
  B Yes, she do / does.

should/shouldn't

should/shouldn't	
Affirmative	**Negative**
I / You / He / She / It / We / They should be careful on the beach.	I / You / He / She / It / We / They should not (shouldn't) swim in cold water.

- We use **should** and **shouldn't** to give advice and say that we think something is a good or bad idea.
  You should put cold water on a burn.
- **Should** is the same for all persons. We use an **infinitive** without **to** after **should**.
  He should help his parents with the housework.

must/mustn't

must/mustn't	
Affirmative	**Negative**
I / You / He / She / It / We / They must drive on the left in the UK.	I / You / He / She / It / We / They must not (mustn't) swim when there is a red flag.

- We use **must** and **mustn't** to give strong advice and talk about rules.
  You must watch this TV programme; it's great.
  You must be 17 to drive a car.
- **Mustn't** means that something isn't allowed.
  You mustn't use your phone in the cinema.
- **Must** is the same for all persons. We use an **infinitive** without **to** after **must**.
  He must remember to take his medicine every day.

Zero conditional

Action/Situation: present simple	Result: present simple
If a bee stings you,	it hurts.
Result: present simple	**Action/Situation:** present simple
It hurts	if a bee stings you.

- We use the zero conditional to talk about situations and their results that are always true.
  If you heat water to 100 °C, it boils.
  When you sprain your ankle, it usually bruises.
- We use a comma to separate the two clauses when the action/situation clause comes first.
  If you work hard, you get results.

First conditional

Action/Situation: present simple	Result: will + infinitive
If we see a jaguar,	we'll take a photo.
Result: will + infinitive	**Action/Situation:** present simple
We'll take a photo	if we see a jaguar.

- We use the first conditional to talk about possible situations in the future and their results.
  If we pass all our exams, we'll have a party.
  You'll lose your teeth if you eat too much sugar.
- We use a comma to separate the two clauses if the action/situation clause comes first.
  If it's good weather tomorrow, we'll go to the park.

should/shouldn't and must/mustn't

1 **Complete the sentences with *should* or *shouldn't* and the verbs in the box.**

> go (x2)   open   stay   wear (x2)

1 It's cold today. You ___should wear___ a warm coat.

2 People say there are sharks in the sea. You _____ swimming.

3 It's raining. You _____ your umbrella.

4 I've got an exam tomorrow. I _____ up late.

5 **A** I've got toothache.

   B You _____ to the dentist.

6 **A** These new shoes are too small for me.

   B You _____ them!

2 **Complete the sentences with *must* or *mustn't* and the verb in brackets.**

1 You _mustn't laugh_ at other students in class. (laugh)

2 You _____ early to get to school on time. (get up)

3 You _____ sandwiches in the classroom. It isn't allowed. (eat)

4 You _____ loudly in the cinema. (talk)

5 You _____ on the chairs. (stand)

6 You _____ your teeth every day. (clean)

3 **Complete the text with *must* or *mustn't* and the verbs in the box.**

> climb   look   ~~swim~~   take   walk   wear

My grandma always thinks of the bad things that can happen to me! When I go to the beach, she says I
¹ _mustn't swim_ in the sea because it's dirty, I
² _____ sandals on the beach because there's a lot of broken glass and I ³ _____ out for sharks in the water! When I go to the mountains, she says I ⁴ _____ near animals that bite or sting, I ⁵ _____ my phone with me so she can ring me and I ⁶ _____ any mountains in case I break my leg!

Zero conditional

4 **Match 1–6 with a–f.**

1 If it rains,   [c]

2 When you read books,   [ ]

3 If my friend is feeling sad,   [ ]

4 When a snake bites you,   [ ]

5 You make the colour green   [ ]

6 If I don't understand something in class,   [ ]

a I try to make her laugh.

b if you mix yellow and blue.

c the grass gets wet.

d you learn things.

e I ask my teacher for help.

f you need to go to hospital.

First conditional

5 **Circle the correct options.**

1 If *you go* / *you'll go* online, I / *I'll* show you my new website.

2 *We* / *We'll* learn about which plants are dangerous if *we go* / *we'll go* to the classes.

3 If *they swim* / *they'll swim* in the sea at night, *they are* / *they'll be* in danger.

4 If you *don't come* / *won't come*, *I'm not* / *I won't be* your friend any more!

5 If *he sees* / *he'll see* a tarantula, *he's* / *he'll be* frightened!

6 **Complete the conditional sentences with the correct form of the verbs in the box.**

> call   eat   not go   not have got   ~~take~~

1 If the computer doesn't work, I ___'ll take___ it to the shop.

2 Sally will play games online if she _____ any homework.

3 They _____ us if they are late.

4 If Harry doesn't get the job, he _____ on holiday.

5 If you _____ something, you'll feel better.

Present perfect: affirmative and negative

Affirmative	Negative
I / You / We / They have ('ve) finished.	I / You / We / They have not (haven't) finished.
He / She / It has ('s) finished.	He / She / It has not (hasn't) finished.

- We use the present perfect to talk about actions with a present result and actions within an unfinished time period.
  I've found my favourite hat!
  Logan hasn't been to the dentist this year.
- To form affirmative sentences, use **subject** + *have/has* + **past participle**.
  I've burnt my hand.
- To form negative sentences, we put *n't* (*not*) after *have/has* and before the past participle. *Not* is usually contracted.
  Smartphones haven't replaced human interaction completely.
- Most verbs in the past participle form end in *-ed*.
  want – wanted   need – needed   play – played
- For verbs ending in *-e*, add *-d*.
  love – loved   hope – hoped   phone – phoned
- For verbs ending in **consonant** + *-y*, remove the final *-y* and add *-ied*.
  study – studied   try – tried   copy – copied
- For verbs ending in **consonant** + **vowel** + **consonant**, double the final consonant and add *-ed*.
  slip – slipped   travel – travelled   drop – dropped
- Some past participles are irregular and don't follow any pattern.
  see – seen   find – found   put – put
- See the irregular verbs list on page 111.

will/won't, may and might

will/won't	
Affirmative	**Negative**
I / You / He / She / It / We / They will ('ll) survive.	I / You / He / She / It / We / They will not (won't) survive.

- We use *will* and *won't* to make certain predictions about the future.
  Computers will control our lives in the future.
  The laptop will help me with my homework.

will/won't	
Question	**Short answer**
Will I / you / he / she / it / we / they survive?	Yes, I / you / he / she / it / we / they will. No, I / you / he / she / it / we / they won't.

- To form questions, we change the order of *will* and the subject.
  Will we travel in cars in the future?

may and *might*	
Affirmative	**Negative**
I / You / He / She / It / We / They may have a flying car.	I / You / He / She / It / We / They may not have a flying car.
I / You / He / She / It / We / They might have a flying car.	I / You / He / She / It / We / They might not have a flying car.

- We use *may* and *might* to make uncertain predictions about the future.
  Rhinos may become extinct in the future; no one knows for sure.
  I might go to Bridget's house this weekend; I don't know yet.

Infinitive of purpose

- We use *to* + **infinitive** to express a purpose for doing something.
  I use a car to get to work.
  She bought a tablet to watch videos when she travels.
  They saved money to pay for the wedding.
  (NOT *They saved money for pay for the wedding.*)

Present perfect: affirmative and negative

1 Complete the table with the past participle of the verbs in the box.

> change   drop   plan   study   try   ~~upload~~

add -d or -ed	remove -y, add -ied	double final consonant, add -ed
1 _uploaded_	3 _____	5 _____
2 _____	4 _____	6 _____

2 Write the past participle of the verbs.

1 have ___had___
2 do _____
3 ride _____
4 write _____
5 forget _____
6 see _____

3 Complete the sentences with the correct form of *have*.

1 I __'ve__ joined an online club at school.
2 Ava _____ fallen off her bike.
3 Luke _____ broken his wrist.
4 We _____ sent them a message.
5 My brother _____ won an internet competition.
6 Laptops _____ made homework easier!

4 Complete the sentences with the present perfect form of the verbs in brackets.

1 I think I __'ve lost__ my new phone. (lose)
2 I can't use my laptop because I _____ my password! (forget)
3 My brother _____ his bed this morning. (not make)
4 Ruth _____ her ankle! (break)
5 My grandad _____ me a new computer! (buy)
6 My teacher says smartphones _____ how we speak to each other. (change)

will/won't, may and might

5 Complete the text with *will* and the verbs in the box.

> be (x2)   do   ~~go~~   study   work

In the future, I think I [1]__'ll go__ to university and I [2]_____ computer technology. I think that computer technology [3]_____ very important in the future because there [4]_____ a lot of new developments in science and technology. Then I think I [5]_____ research at a university in America or Australia. After that, I think I [6]_____ in a company which invents new technology.

6 (Circle) the correct options.

1 In the future, children *will* / (*won't*) go to school because they'll study at home.
2 Luke *might* / *will* be in his bedroom, but I don't know. Go and look.
3 We *will* / *won't* all have electric cars in 100 years because there won't be any petrol.
4 I *will* / *may* meet Tom tonight, but I haven't decided yet.
5 The library *won't* / *may not* let you borrow more than four books – I'm not sure. Let's ask.
6 People won't work in factories in the future because robots *will* / *won't* do all of the work.

Infinitive of purpose

7 Complete the text with the infinitive of purpose. Use the verbs in the box.

> ~~buy~~   change   have   show   speak   take

Yesterday my mum went shopping [1]__to buy__ a new phone. I went with her [2]_____ my new tablet for a different one because it was broken. When we were going home, we stopped at a café [3]_____ a coffee and then we stopped again [4]_____ to some neighbours we saw in the park. Mum used her new phone [5]_____ some photos of us [6]_____ my dad at home. It was really late when we got home, but my dad loved the photos!

Present perfect for experience

Affirmative	Negative
I / You / We / They have ('ve) seen this film.	I / You / We / They have not (haven't) seen this film.
He / She / It has ('s) seen this film.	He / She / It has not (hasn't) seen this film.

- We use the present perfect to talk about experiences.
  He's visited every country in Europe.
  Jayden and Layla haven't met Mia.

Question	Short answer
Have I / you / we / they seen this film?	Yes, I / you / we / they have. No, I / you / we / they haven't.
Has he / she / it seen this film?	Yes, he / she / it has. No, he / she / it hasn't.

- We form **Yes/No** questions with **have/has** + **subject** + **past participle**.
  Has your mum been to Spain?
- We repeat **have/has** in short answers.
  A *Have you tried Turkish food?*
  B *Yes, I have.*

- When we talk about experience, we can use **ever** in questions to mean 'at any time', and **never** in affirmative sentences to mean 'at no time'.
  Have you ever seen a crocodile in real life?
  I've never travelled outside of my country.

Reflexive pronouns

I – myself	I saw **myself** on TV.
you – yourself	You saw **yourself** on TV.
he – himself	He saw **himself** on TV.
she – herself	She saw **herself** on TV.
it – itself	It saw **itself** on TV.
we – ourselves	We saw **ourselves** on TV.
you (plural) – yourselves	You saw **yourselves** on TV.
they – themselves	They saw **themselves** on TV.

- We use reflexive pronouns when the subject and the object of a sentence are the same, or to emphasise the subject of an action.
  My dad talks to himself when he's nervous.
  I made dinner myself in the end because Dad was late.
- The pronoun usually goes directly after the verb.
  We enjoyed ourselves at Liam's birthday party.
  (NOT *We enjoyed at Liam's birthday party ourselves.*)

Indefinite pronouns

	People	Things	Places
Some-: to talk about one person / thing / place in a positive sentence	**Someone / Somebody** called me earlier.	I want **something** to eat.	I want to go **somewhere** hot on holiday.
Every-: to talk about all people, things or places	**Everyone / Everybody** likes chocolate.	**Everything** in your flat is beautiful.	I've been **everywhere** in London.
Any-: to talk about one person, thing or place in a negative sentence or question	I don't know **anyone** / **anybody** at this party.	I don't have **anything** to wear to the party.	I don't want to go **anywhere** tonight.
No-: to indicate no people, things or places	**No one / Nobody** called me yesterday.	**Nothing** happened last night.	**Nowhere** is open for dinner tonight.

- We use indefinite pronouns to talk about people, things and places without specifying those people, things and places.
- Indefinite pronouns take a singular verb.
  Everyone is excited about the wedding. (NOT *Everyone are excited about the wedding.*)
- We usually use an affirmative verb with **no one**, **nothing** and **nowhere**.
  There's nothing to do here! (NOT *There isn't nothing to do here!*)
- We usually use a negative verb with **anyone**, **anything** and **anywhere**.
  I haven't got anything to do today. (NOT *I've got anything to do today.*)

LANGUAGE PRACTICE

Present perfect for experience

1 Complete the sentences with the correct words.

> 've ever has have haven't never

1 I __'ve__ flown on a plane.
2 He's _____ been to Iceland, but he wants to go in the future.
3 A _____ you ever ridden a camel?
   B No, I _____ .
4 A Has your grandad _____ used a laptop?
   B Yes, he _____ !

2 Write questions and short answers with the present perfect and *ever*.

1 you / climb / a mountain / ?
   Have you ever climbed a mountain?
   No, I __haven't__ .
2 Christina / sprain / her ankle / ?
   _____
   Yes, she _____ .
3 Tony / eat / Japanese food / ?
   _____
   No, he _____ .
4 your parents / travel / to a different country / ?
   _____
   No, they _____ .
5 your sister / learn / a new language / ?
   _____
   Yes, she _____ .
6 you / spend / too much money / ?
   _____
   Yes, I _____ .

3 Underline and correct one mistake in each sentence.

1 Have <u>ever you</u> driven a car? __you ever__
2 I've never invent anything! _____
3 Has your brother ever win a prize? _____
4 She haven't been to a different country. _____
5 I haven't never seen a waterfall. _____

Reflexive pronouns

4 Circle the correct options.

1 She wrote the song (herself)/ himself.
2 He only thinks about herself / himself.
3 People with talent usually believe in yourself / themselves.
4 My dad says we should always defend ourselves / themselves.
5 I taught myself / himself how to play chess.
6 The laptop switches itself / himself off when you stop using it.

5 Complete the sentences with the correct reflexive pronouns.

1 Do you like looking at __yourself__ in the mirror?
2 Monica taught _____ to play the guitar.
3 I don't like taking photos of _____ because I look terrible in them!
4 These lights turn _____ on when it's dark.
5 Jack hurt _____ when he was climbing.
6 We enjoyed _____ at the concert.

Indefinite pronouns

6 Circle the correct options.

1 Someone /(No one) lives in that house – the last family moved out two weeks ago.
2 There's something / nothing better than helping other people.
3 My uncle loves travelling. He's been everywhere / nowhere except Australia and New Zealand!
4 Somewhere / Someone told me it's better to dress smartly if you want to make a good impression.
5 I've got nothing / no one to tell you.
6 She hasn't got anywhere / nowhere to stay when she begins her new job in London.

going to

Affirmative	Negative
I am ('m) going to dance.	I am ('m) not going to dance.
You / We / They are ('re) going to dance.	You / We / They are not (aren't) going to dance.
He / She / It is ('s) going to dance.	He / She / It is not (isn't) going to dance.

- We use **going to** to talk about future plans and intentions.
  I'm going to work in another country in the future.
- To form the affirmative, we use **be** + **going to** + **infinitive**.
  We're going to travel around Europe before university.
- To form the negative, we use **be** + **not** + **going to** + **infinitive**.
  Ryan isn't going to study French in France.

Question	Short answer
Am I going to dance?	Yes, I am. No, I'm not.
Are you / we / they going to dance?	Yes, you / we / they are. No, you / we / they aren't.
Is he / she / it going to dance?	Yes, he / she / it is. No, he / she / it isn't.

- We form questions with **be** before the subject.
  Are they going to get married this year?
- We repeat **be** in short answers.
  A Are you going to learn the keyboard?
  B Yes, I am.

will and going to

- We use **will** for predictions and **going to** for future plans and intentions.
  Lidia will be the best singer in the school show.
  We're going to write the school play next year – Mr Newsome has decided.

Present continuous for future

- We use the present continuous to talk about fixed arrangements in the future, especially plans we've agreed with other people.
  I'm meeting my friends at 8 pm tomorrow. We're seeing a concert.
  We're having lunch with my aunt next Saturday.
- We often use future time expressions such as **tonight**, **tomorrow**, **this weekend**, **this summer**, **next week**, **next month** and **after class**/**school** with the present continuous for future.
  Aria and I are practising for the school show this weekend.

Present simple for future

- We use the present simple to talk about scheduled events in the future.
  The concert starts at 10 pm tomorrow. It finishes at midnight.
  My plane leaves tomorrow morning at nine.
  Their train arrives at 8.45 in the morning.
  Our summer holidays start on 24 June.

LANGUAGE PRACTICE

going to

1 Complete the sentences with the correct form of *going to* and the verbs in the box.

> buy   not go   not work   perform   ~~study~~

1 I *'m going to study* music and dance at university.
2 Agnieszka _____ in her dad's shop this summer.
3 My brother _____ in a musical next week.
4 My parents _____ a new house next year.
5 We _____ to summer camp this year.

2 Write questions with *going to*. Use the words in brackets.

1 What *are you going to do* (you / do) this summer?
2 Where _____ (Tina / work) next year?
3 When _____ (your parents / start) their salsa classes?
4 What _____ (brother / do) at the weekend?
5 _____ (you / learn) the guitar next year?
6 _____ (your sister / buy) tickets for the pop concert tomorrow?

will and *going to*

3 Decide if the sentences are predictions or intentions. Then circle the best options.

1 I think you *will* / *are going to* need an umbrella today because it might rain.
2 We *will* / *are going to* buy the tickets for the show tomorrow.
3 They *will* / *are going to* watch ballroom dancing tomorrow night.
4 I think it *will* / *is going to* be difficult to find a good job in the future.
5 I'm sure you *will* / *are going to* pass the exam – with a bit of luck.

Present continuous for future

4 Write present continuous sentences about the people in the table.

	Jess	Marta and Adam
tonight	(1) study for a test	(2) go for a pizza with their friends
this weekend	(3) watch ballet	(4) go to a concert

1 *Jess is studying for a test tonight.*
2 _____
3 _____
4 _____

5 Complete the conversation with the present continuous form of the verbs in the box.

> ~~do~~   go (x2)   have   make   meet

Mia What [1] *are you doing* tonight?
Mason I [2] _____ dinner at Joss's house at about six, but nothing after that. Why?
Mia Ava and I [3] _____ breakdancing in the park.
Mason Sounds interesting. What time [4] _____ you _____ to the park?
Mia Well, the first dancers are always there at eight, but I [5] _____ Ava at 7.30 in the café in front of the park first. Why don't you ask Joss to come, too?
Mason He can't. He [6] _____ a video with his classmates for a school project.

Present simple for future

6 Complete the sentences with the present simple form of the verbs in brackets.

1 The bus *leaves* at 3 pm this afternoon. (leave)
2 When _____ this year's opera programme _____ ? (begin)
3 The tap dancing class tomorrow _____ for more than three hours! (last)
4 My brother _____ his first concert next week! (have)
5 The show _____ at about 10 pm. (finish)
6 When _____ the new theatre _____ ? (open)

LANGUAGE BANK

STARTER

Vocabulary
Free time and hobbies

> a bike ride   a blog   books/magazines
> cakes/videos   friends   an instrument
> music   online   photos   shopping   songs

Sport

> athletics   basketball   gymnastics   hockey
> rugby   sailing   swimming   table tennis
> volleyball   windsurfing

Personal possessions

> bus pass   camera   headphones   keys
> laptop   money   passport   phone
> portable charger   tablet

Language in action
love, like, don't mind, hate + -ing
have got

Writing
Useful language
Using commas and apostrophes
We use apostrophes:
• for contractions/short forms: *name's*
• to show possession: *My cat's name is Tiger.*
We use commas to indicate a pause: *I live with my mum and dad, my grandma and my cat.*

UNIT 1

Vocabulary
TV shows

> cartoon   chat show   comedy   cookery show
> documentary   drama   game show
> on-demand series   reality show   soap opera
> sports show   the news

Making movies

> actor   camera operator   costume
> (digital) camera   director   lights
> make-up artist   script   set   sound engineer

Language in action
Present continuous
Present simple and present continuous
Adverbs of manner

Speaking
Everyday English
Actually
It's really cool!
Let's see.
Well?

Useful language
Do you like …?
I like/love/hate/prefer watching …
I'm not really into it/them.
It's great/good/not bad/awful.
What do you think of …?

Writing
Useful language
Giving similar or contrasting information
and to add similar information
but to show different information
or when there is a choice of two or more things

LANGUAGE BANK

UNIT 2

Vocabulary
The weather

> cloudy cold dry foggy hot
> icy rainy snowy stormy sunny warm
> wet windy

Useful objects

> blanket bowl comb cup fork
> hairbrush knife lamp mirror pillow
> plate scissors spoon toothbrush

Language in action
Past simple
there was/there were

Speaking
Everyday English
Nothing much.
Sounds good!
That's a shame.
You learn something new every day!

Useful language
How was your weekend?
It was (OK/good/great/amazing/awful), thanks.
What about you?
What did you do?
What was the weather like?
Where did you stay?

Writing
Useful language
Writing an account of a journey
At first, …
Finally, …
(He) set off on …
There were a lot of problems.
The weather was …

UNIT 3

Vocabulary
Adjectives of feeling

> afraid angry bored embarrassed
> excited lonely nervous surprised tired
> worried upset

Prepositions of movement

> across along between down
> into off out of over past through
> under up

Language in action
Past continuous: affirmative and negative
Past continuous: questions
Past simple and past continuous

Speaking
Everyday English
Go on.
No idea.
What a great story!
You're kidding!

Useful language
Guess what happened (yesterday)?
It happened to …
Really?
That's amazing/incredible!
What was (he) doing (in) …?

Writing
Useful language
Sequencing words and phrases
A few minutes later, …
At first, …
In the end, …
One night last summer, …
Suddenly, …
The next morning, …

LANGUAGE BANK

UNIT 4

Vocabulary
Money verbs

> borrow   change   cost   earn
> lend   owe   pay   save   sell   spend

Caring jobs

> carer   charity worker   firefighter   lawyer
> lifeguard   nurse   paramedic   police officer
> refuse collector   surgeon   vet   volunteer

Language in action
could
Comparative and superlative adjectives
too, too much, too many
(*not*) *enough* + noun

Speaking

Everyday English
cute
I owe you one.
There you are.
What's up?

Useful language
Could you do me a favour?
I'm sorry, I can't.
It depends.
Sure.
Would you mind … + *-ing* … ?

Writing
Useful language
Giving your opinion
First of all, …
I believe that …
In my opinion, …
Personally, I think that …
To sum up, …

UNIT 5

Vocabulary
Furniture

> armchair   bookcase   carpet   ceiling
> chest of drawers   cupboard   desk   floor
> fridge   picture   shelves   sink   wardrobe

Household chores

> clean (the kitchen)   do the ironing
> do the washing   do the washing-up
> empty (the washing machine)
> load the dishwasher   make your bed
> tidy up (the living room)   vacuum (the carpet)

Language in action
(*not*) *as* + adjective + *as*
(*not*) + adjective + *enough*
have to/don't have to

Speaking

Everyday English
I'm not convinced.
It looks awesome!
Me neither.
Me too.

Useful language
at the bottom/top
in the background
on the left/right
What's that … ?

Writing
Useful language
Adding information
also
as well
as well as
too

LANGUAGE BANK

UNIT 6

Vocabulary
Accidents and injuries

> be bitten   be stung   break   bruise
> burn   cut   fall off   hit   scratch   slip
> sprain   trip over

Parts of the body

> cheek   chest   chin   elbow
> forehead   heel   knee   neck
> shoulder   teeth   toe   wrist

Language in action
should/shouldn't and *must/mustn't*
Zero conditional and first conditional

Speaking
Everyday English
Awesome
buddies
I'll give it/them a go.
Nice one

Useful language
How about + *-ing* … ?
Make sure you don't …
Why don't you … ?
You should definitely …

Writing
Useful language
Giving advice
I'd say …
If you ask me, …
Make sure …
That's why …

UNIT 7

Vocabulary
Communication and technology

> app   chip   device   download   emoji
> message   screen   social media
> software   upload   video chat

Getting around

> catch/get/take   get into/out of
> get off/get on   go by   go on

Language in action
Present perfect: affirmative and negative
will/won't, may and *might*
Infinitive of purpose

Speaking
Everyday English
Got that?
Like this?
Not quite.
That's it.

Useful language
Before you start, …
It's really important that …
Make sure that …
Remember to check that …

Writing
Useful language
Giving examples
for example
for instance
such as
Adding more information
In addition, …
What's more, …

LANGUAGE BANK

UNIT 8

Vocabulary
Exceptional jobs and qualities

> athlete   businessman/businesswoman
> composer   inventor   mathematician
> scientist   surgeon   writer

> creativity   determination   intelligence
> skill   strength   talent

Phrasal verbs: achievement

> carry on   come up with   give up
> keep up with   look up to   set off   set up
> show off   take part in   work out

Language in action
Present perfect for experience
Reflexive pronouns
Indefinite pronouns

Speaking
Everyday English
Tell me more.
that sort of thing
the main thing is
you see

Useful language
I'm passionate about …
I've had plenty of experience of …
I've learned how to …
I've learned the basics of …

Writing
Useful language
Talking about achievements
after a lot of effort
How did I manage it?
My advice to you is …
My greatest achievement is …

UNIT 9

Vocabulary
Musical instruments and genres

> bass   drums   guitar   keyboard
> microphone   saxophone   trumpet   violin

> classical   folk   hip-hop   jazz   reggae   rock

Dance styles

> ballet dancing   ballroom dancing   breakdance
> country dancing   disco dancing   modern dance
> salsa dancing   swing   tap dancing   zumba

Language in action
going to
will and *going to*
Present continuous for future
Present simple for future

Speaking
Everyday English
all day long
Never mind.
That's a pity.
That's no good.
What are you up to?

Useful language
Do you fancy …?
I'd love to, but …
I'm afraid …
(She's) welcome to …
Thanks for asking, though.
Would you like to …?

Writing
Useful language
Writing a review
All in all, …
If you love (dance), this (show) is a must-see.
I was impressed by …
On the downside, …
The highlight of the show is …

IRREGULAR VERBS

Infinitive	Past simple	Past participle
be	was / were	been
beat	beat	beaten
become	became	become
begin	began	begun
break	broke	broken
bring	brought	brought
build	built	built
burn	burnt / burned	burnt / burned
buy	bought	bought
catch	caught	caught
choose	chose	chosen
come	came	come
cost	cost	cost
cut	cut	cut
do	did	done
draw	drew	drawn
drink	drank	drunk
drive	drove	driven
eat	ate	eaten
fall	fell	fallen
feed	fed	fed
feel	felt	felt
fight	fought	fought
find	found	found
fly	flew	flown
forget	forgot	forgotten
get	got	got
give	gave	given
go	went	gone
grow	grew	grown
hang	hung	hung
have	had	had
hear	heard	heard
hide	hid	hidden
hit	hit	hit
hold	held	held
keep	kept	kept

Infinitive	Past simple	Past participle
know	knew	known
leave	left	left
lend	lent	lent
lose	lost	lost
make	made	made
meet	met	met
pay	paid	paid
put	put	put
read	read	read
ride	rode	ridden
ring	rang	rung
run	ran	run
say	said	said
see	saw	seen
sell	sold	sold
send	sent	sent
set	set	set
show	showed	shown
shut	shut	shut
sing	sang	sung
sit	sat	sat
sleep	slept	slept
speak	spoke	spoken
spend	spent	spent
stand	stood	stood
swim	swam	swum
take	took	taken
teach	taught	taught
tell	told	told
think	thought	thought
throw	threw	thrown
understand	understood	understood
wake	woke	woken
wear	wore	worn
win	won	won
write	wrote	written

Acknowledgements

The authors and publishers acknowledge the following sources of copyright material and are grateful for the permissions granted. While every effort has been made, it has not always been possible to identify the sources of all the material used, or to trace all copyright holders. If any omissions are brought to our notice, we will be happy to include the appropriate acknowledgements on reprinting and in the next update to the digital edition, as applicable.

Key: SU = Starter Unit, U = Unit.

Text

U2: Text about Dervla Murphy. Copyright © Eland Publishing Ltd. Reproduced with permission; U8: Text about Jacob Barnett. Copyright © Kristine Barnett. Reproduced with kind permission of Kristine Barnett; Text about Aaron Fotheringham. Copyright © WCMX International, LLC. Reproduced with permission; Text about Bethany Hamilton. Copyright © Bethany Hamilton. Reproduced with permission.

Photography

The following photographs are sourced from Getty Images.

SU: Westend61; Sharlotta/iStock/Getty Images Plus; Imgorthand/E+; Tetra Images; Denise Crew; gbh007/iStock/Getty Images Plus; Compassionate Eye Foundation/DigitalVision; aluxum/E+; FatCamera/E+; Creative Crop/Photodisc; pagadesign/E+; Maurizio Cigognetti/Photographer's Choice; Pakorn Polachai/EyeEm; VAKSMANV/iStock/Getty Images Plus; Alexandr Dubovitskiy/iStock/Getty Images Plus; tovovan/iStock/Getty Images Plus; kotomiti/iStock/Getty Images Plus; nidwlw/iStock/Getty Images Plus; Jeffrey Coolidge/DigitalVision; D'Franc Photography/Moment Open; Ariel Skelley/DigitalVision; Kevin Dodge/Corbis; Feverpitched/iStock/Getty Images Plus; U1: Tetra Images; Gusztav Gallo/EyeEm; LueratSatichob/DigitalVision Vectors; PeopleImages/iStock/Getty Images Plus; Science Photo Library/Getty Images Plus; 36clicks/iStock/Getty Images Plus; Elva Etienne/Moment; ollo/iStock Unreleased; JGI/Jamie Grill; drbimages/E+; Westend61; PhotoAlto/Odilon Dimier; U2: alubalish/iStock/Getty Images Plus; Imgorthand/E+; Tim Graham/The Image Bank; stephen johnson/iStock/Getty Images Plus; Rolf Bruderer; Daniel Friend/iStock/Getty Images Plus; Lars Thulin, Johner; Tetra Images; Layland Masuda/Moment Open; Rob Lewine; NUTAN/Gamma-Rapho; Tuomas Lehtinen/Moment Open; coco lang; jordieasy/iStock/Getty Images Plus; Lovely Edeza/EyeEm; RinoCdZ/E+; xenicx/iStock/Getty Images Plus; Caiaimage/Paul Bradbury; Leemage/Universal Images Group; Stígur Már Karlsson/Heimsmyndir/E+; U3: Betsie Van Der Meer/DigitalVision; Michael Echteld/Moment; @ Didier Marti/Moment; Table Mesa Prod./Photolibrary; gradyreese/E+; Norbert Schaefer/Corbis; DAJ; Hero Images; Comstock/Stockbyte; Erik Von Weber/The Image Bank; Patrick Schwalb/Picture Press; yaoinlove/iStock/Getty Images Plus; Adriana Varela Photography/Moment; AJ_Watt/E+; Nico De Pasquale Photography/Moment; perets/iStock/Getty Images Plus; whitemay/iStock/Getty Images Plus; Pete Saloutos/Image Source; Cultura RM Exclusive/Alan Graf/Cultura Exclusive; krblokhin/iStock/Getty Images Plus; Jupiterimages/Goodshoot; mtreasure/iStock/Getty Images Plus; LeventKonuk/iStock/Getty Images Plus; U4: bluecinema/iStock/Getty Images Plus; Tanya St/iStock/Getty Images Plus; Lokibaho/iStock Unreleased; kali9/iStock/Getty Images Plus; Yellow Dog Productions/The Image Bank; Ljupco/iStock/Getty Images Plus; drbimages/E+; Photo_Concepts/Cultura; Juanmonino/iStock/Getty Images Plus; Comstock Images/Stockbyte; moodboard/Cultura; Jamie Kingham/Image Source; Terry Vine/DigitalVision; jabejon/iStock/Getty Images Plus; Steve Debenport/E+; DGLimages/iStock/Getty Images Plus; rubberball; Marc Romanelli; FangXiaNuo/E+; U5: Dorling Kindersley; YangYin/E+; Jena Ardell/Moment; Julija Svetlova/EyeEm; Grant Faint/The Image Bank; clu/iStock/Getty Images Plus; De Agostini/Al Pagani/De Agostini Picture Library/Getty Images Plus; Nongnuch Leelaphasuk/EyeEm; Sergey05/iStock/Getty Images Plus; Kate Davis/Dorling Kindersley; Grafimania/iStock/Getty Images Plus; JazzIRT/E+; Mark Griffin/EyeEm; Skadr/iStock/Getty Images Plus; acilo/iStock/Getty Images Plus; Elisa Bonomini/EyeEm; Fuse/Corbis; bluestocking/iStock/Getty Images Plus; Carol Yepes/Moment; Ridofranz/iStock/Getty Images Plus; Hero Images; TanyaLovus/iStock/Getty Images Plus; penkanya/iStock/Getty Images Plus; Simon Watson/The Image Bank; Juanmonino/E+; Mehmet Hilmi Barcin/iStock/Getty Images Plus; Ismailciydem/iStock/Getty Images Plus; SolStock/E+; Hoxton/Martin Barraud; Westend61; PaulVinten/iStock/Getty Images Plus; U6: Pixel_Pig/E+; yuoak/DigitalVision Vectors; Roger Eritja/Oxford Scientific; Will & Deni McIntyre/Corbis Documentary; D. Sharon Pruitt Pink Sherbet Photography/Moment; Siberian Photographer/iStock/Getty Images Plus; Janista/iStock/Getty Images Plus; Ecelop/iStock/Getty Images Plus; designalldone/DigitalVision Vectors; Evgenii_Bobrov/iStock/Getty Images Plus; Creative Crop/Photodisc; JackF/iStock/Getty Images Plus; AH86/iStock/Getty Images Plus; Hero Images; Andreas Strauss/LOOK-foto; Westend61; U7: aphichart/iStock/Getty Images Plus; Colin Hawkins/Stone; Westend61; Monkey Business Images; Andrew Bret Wallis/DigitalVision; yuoak/DigitalVision Vectors; beyhanyazar/iStock/Getty Images Plus; Betsie Van Der Meer/Taxi; Ronnie Kaufman/DigitalVision; Valeriy_G/iStock/Getty Images Plus; Ryan McVay/Valueline; izusek/E+; BJI/Lane Oatey; Mlenny/E+; Francis Dean/Corbis News; kate_sept2004/E+; U8: D Dipasupil/WireImage; James Devaney/Getty Images Entertainment; Johann Mouchel/Icon Sport; jabejon/iStock/Getty Images Plus; asiseeit/E+; MikeCherim/iStock/Getty Images Plus; Vladimir Godnik; Image Source/DigitalVision; FluxFactory/E+; Morsa Images/DigitalVision; piamphoto/iStock/Getty Images Plus; GUSTOIMAGES/Science Photo Library/Getty Images Plus; Sion Touhig/Getty Images News; Sion Touhig/Getty Images News; Hill Street Studios/DigitalVision; Tatiana Mezhenina/iStock/Getty Images Plus; Tyler D. Rickenbach/Aurora Photos; U9: Arthur Baensch/Corbis; Jon Feingersh Photography Inc/DigitalVision; urbancow/iStock/Getty Images Plus; Hill Street Studios/DigitalVision; kali9/E+; Education Images/Universal Images Group; Laures/iStock/Getty Images Plus; Cimmerian/E+; simon2579/DigitalVision Vectors; JackF/iStock/Getty Images Plus; Dorling Kindersley; Hemera Technologies/PhotoObjects.net; lcodacci/E+; Seamind Panadda/EyeEm; Gannet77/E+; Steve Debenport/E+; Monkey Business Images; Inti St Clair; eclipse_images/E+; Rubberball/Nicole Hill; Ryan Smith/Corbis; recep-bg/E+; Jena Ardell/Moment; Erik Isakson; Paul Bradbury/OJO Images; PeopleImages/E+.

The following photographs are sourced from other libraries/sources.

U2: Copyright © Eland Publishing Ltd.; **U8:** Copyright © Kristine Barnett; Copyright © Bethany Hamilton; Copyright © WCMX International, LLC.

Illustration

U2, U3: Oliver Flores; **U3, U5, U6:** Alex Herrerias; **U3, U8, U9:** Jose Rubio; **U4, U7, U8, VE5:** Antonio Cuesta.

Typesetting: Blooberry Design

Cover illustration: Collaborate Agency

Audio recordings: Creative Listening

Video production: Lucentum Digital

Freelance editing: Mattew Duffy, Jacqueline French, Melissa Wilson